NAVIGATIO

# VOYAGE OF THE SONORA
# FROM THE 1775 JOURNAL

# The Hon. Daines Barrington


Published by T. C. Russell, San Francisco

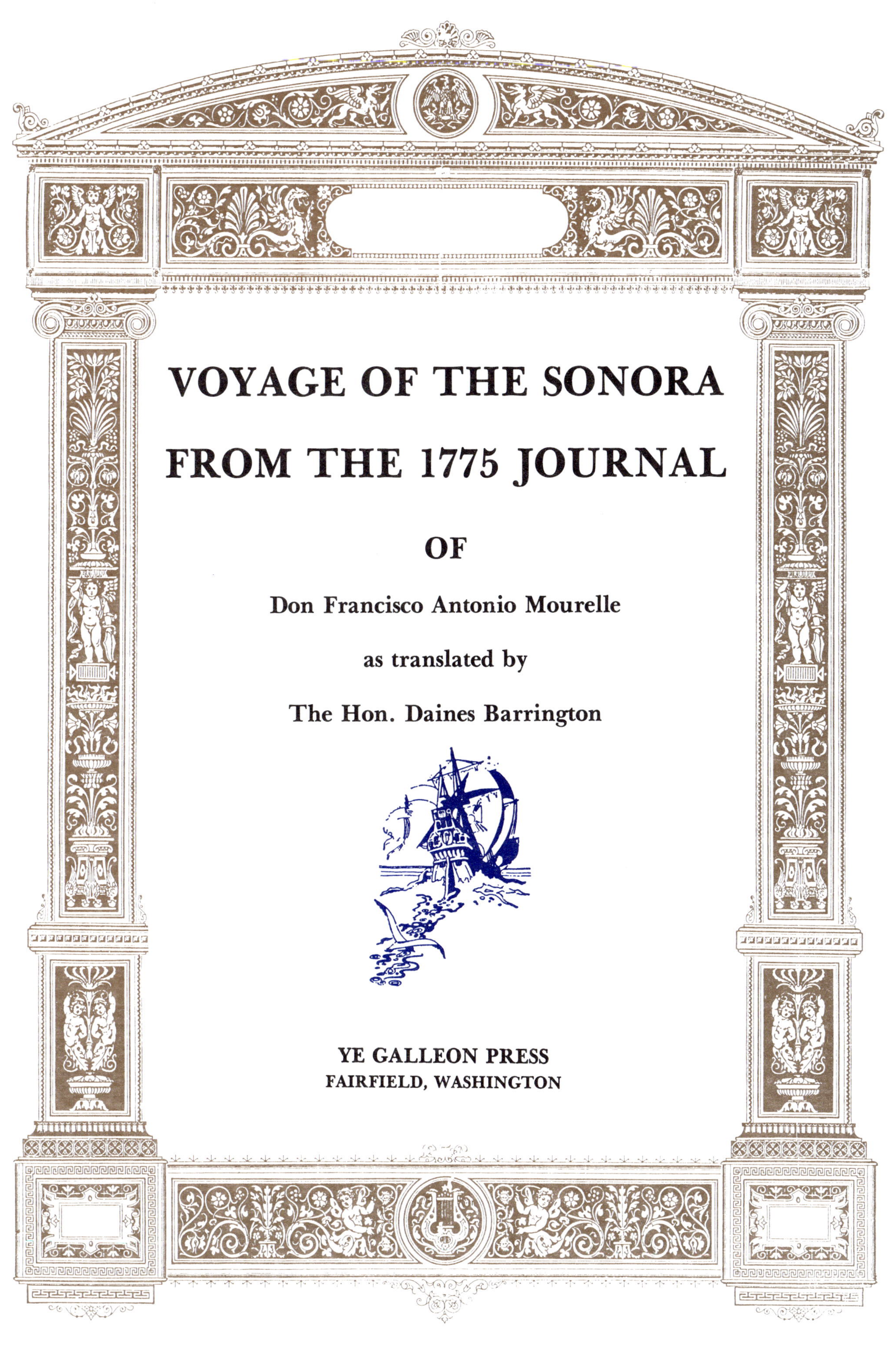

# VOYAGE OF THE SONORA

# FROM THE 1775 JOURNAL

## OF

Don Francisco Antonio Mourelle

as translated by

The Hon. Daines Barrington

YE GALLEON PRESS
FAIRFIELD, WASHINGTON

Of this Edition_______ Copies were printed.

This is Copy Number_______.

Library of Congress Cataloging in Publication Data

Mourelle de la Rua, Francisco Antonio, 1750-1820.
    Voyage of the Sonora from the 1775 journal of Don Francisco Antonio
Mourelle as translated by Daines Barrington.

    Original English ed. published as: Journal of a voyage in 1775. 1780?
    Reprint of the 1920 ed. published by T. C. Russell, San Francisco,
Calif., under title: Voyage of the Sonora in the second Bucareli
expedition. . .
    Bibliography: p.
    Includes index.
    1. Northwest Coast of North America—Discovery and exploration. 2.
Spaniards—Northwest Coast of North America—History—18th century. 3.
Mourelle de la Rua, Francisco Antonio, 1750-1820—Diaries. 4.
Spain—Exploring expeditions. I. Title.
F851.5.M68              1987            979.5'01            87-6085
ISBN 0-87770-402-3

# CONTENTS

¿ Maurelle ó Mourelle ?

*The correct spelling of the Journalist's surname is, after much investigation, found to be* MOURELLE.
*A change could not, of course, be made in the Journal, and the matter was not fully determined when the Notes were made.*

# Thomas C. Russell, Printer and Publisher

## *by John Barr Tompkins*

SAN FRANCISCO is a city well known for its excellent typographic heritage and for the men who have labored to establish that reputation and who continue to maintain it at the present time.

Concerning most of the printers upon whose works this honor is based, a considerable body of personal data is available. But concerning one of the leading practitioners of the art, Thomas C. Russell, surprisingly little is known.

His place of origin, details of his youth, and the history of his employment prior to his appearance in San Frncisco all remain obscure. Most of what is known of Russell is to be found in and between the lines of his now famous and sought-for reprints of what may best be termed his California "classics" and in his short-lived *The California Reprint*.

Recourse to the early directories of San Francisco proved

useful in shedding light on Russell, although there is still a question as to the date of the first appearance of his name in these sources.

As early as 1883-84, *Langley's Directory* listed a Thomas Russell, printer, at 1032 Market Street. Could this be the Thomas C. Russell whose name appeared in this form for the first time in the directory of 1887, with an address of 216 Golden Gate Avenue? At any rate, from 1887 forward, the name of Thomas C. Russell appeared with more or less regularity, and his various roles in the world of book production may be followed with ease, if not in close detail.

In 1888, Russell was listed as compositor with the firm of Filmer and Stiller Electro Company; this position he kept through the following year and, in 1890, he was listed as a proofreader with Filmer and Rollins. His association with this firm lasted at least until 1891, possibly longer. In 1894, when the directories next mentioned him, Russell was listed as a printer, with no reference to an employer. In the following year, he was listed as a proofreader again and, in 1899, he was still listed in that capacity. It was also in 1899 that the name of his wife Minnie made its first appearance in the directory.

By 1901, Russell was manager of the T.C. Russell Company, a printing establishment at 530 Commercial Street; this firm seems to have lasted through 1902. In 1903, Russell was listed once more as a proofreader, this time with the firm of W.N. Brunt Company on Clay Street.

In 1905, a new note was struck—Russell was listed as proprietor of the Russell Book Company at 22 Seventh Street, dealing in second-hand books. From 1908 until 1910, he appeared once more as a proofreader, this time with Bender Moss Company, publisher of law books.

In 1911, a Russell appeared as a publisher, operating, it would seem, out of his home on Nineteenth Avenue, which was to be his place of business for the balance of his life. This venture into publishing was in connection with *The California Reprint.* A more prophetic title could hardly have been chosen by this man who came to be known chiefly for his reprints of several of the best-known and most reliable works of Californiana.

*The California Reprint* consisted of but two issued (Vol. I, Nos. 1-2, July-August 1911) and totalled but sixteen pages. The first issue carried the following statement by Russell:

> Readers of the Reprint, who may desire to have reprinted anything rare or curious relating to California, are invited to correspond with the Publisher. Book-collectors, who may desire to purchase, sell, or exchange, are also invited to correspond.
>
> A postal card with the sender's name and address, together with his bookseller's, addressed to the Publisher, will insure delivery of the next number of the Reprint.
>
> Advertising rates given on application.

The only advertisements carried in the *Reprint* concerned the books which Russell had for sale or exchange, and his own publication, *Panoramic San Francisco, 1877,* a photographic study of the city looking east and south from California Street hill.

These two items, as well as the eight books to come from Russell's press between 1917 and 1930, are all to be found in the Bancroft Library of the University of California, where the books, at least, have been well used.

In the order of their appearance his reprints were:

McGOWAN, EDWARD. Narrative of Edward McGowan, including a full account of the author's adventures and perils while persecuted by the San Francisco vigilance committee of 1856, together with a report of his trial, which resulted in his acquittal . . . San Francisco, California . . . 1917.
3 p. I., 5-7, viii, 9-240 p. illus., port. 21 i/c cm. "Reprinted line for line and page for page, from the original edition, published by the author in 1857, complete with reproductions, in facsimile, of the original illustrations, cover-page title and title page."

The style of "McGowan" with its red and black title page, Caslon type, head and tail pieces, bound in boards with Irish linen backs and paper label, set the style for all his subsequent productions. The edition consisted of 200 copies.

FORBES, ALEXANDER. California: a history of Upper & Lower California from their first discovery to the present time, comprising an account of the climate, soil, natural productions, agriculture, commerce, &c. A full view of the missionary establishments and condition of the free & domesticated Indians, with an appendix relating to steam-navigation in the Pacific, illustrated with a new map, plans of the harbors and numerous engravings . . . Reprinted page for page, and approsimately line for line, from the original edition, Pub. by Smith, Elder & co., London, 1839, and to which is added a new index. San Francisco, 1919.
10ª, xvi, 372 p. front. (port.) illus., plates, fold. map 276m.

The paper used was Dresden Pamphlet paper, according to Mrs. Barr's *Presses of Northern California*. The edition was of 250 copies.

MOURELLE, ANTONIO FRANCISCO. Voyage of the Sonora in the second Burcareli expedition to explore the northwest coast, survey the port of San Francisco, and found the Franciscan missions and a presidio and pueblo at that port; the journal kept in 1775 on the Sonora, by Don Francisco Antonio Mourelle, the second pilot of the fleet constituting the sea division of the expedition; tr. by the Hon. Daines Barrington from the original Spanish manuscript; reprinted line for line and page for page from Barrington's Miscellanies published in London in 1781, with concise notes showing the voyages of the earliest explorers on the coast, the sea and land expeditions of Galvez and of Bucareli for settling California and for founding missions, and many other interesting notes as well as an entirely new index to both text & notes . . . together with a reproduction of the de la Bodega Spanish Carta general showing Spanish discoveries, etc., on the coast up to 1791 and also a portrait of Sir Daines Barrington. San Francisco, 1920.

xii, 120 p., 1 l. incl. tables. front. (port.) 2 maps (1 fold) 29 cm.

The Mourelle work is decorated on the front cover with a ship of war, and contains both head and tail pieces. It was set in Caslon type, and was bound in the typical Russell manner. The edition was 230 copies.


CLAPPE, LOUISE AMELIA KNAPP. The Shirley letters from California mines in 1851-52; being a series of twenty-three letters from Dame Shirley . . . to her sister in Massachusetts, and now reprinted from the Pioneer Magazine of 1854-55 with synopses of the letters, a foreword, and many typographical and other corrections and emendations . . . together with "An appreciation" by Mrs. M.V.T. Lawrence . . . San Francisco, 1922.

L p., i l., 350 p., i l. col. front., col. plates 24½ cm.

In this work, Russell employed blue and black for the title page, used both head and tail pieces and many initials in the same blue. The plates were hand colored. The edition consisted of 450 copies—200 on Exeter paper, 200 on buff California Bond paper, and 50 on thin buff California Bond paper. The type used was Caslon.

> ROBINSON, ALFRED. Life in California before the conquest; Hispano-Californianas, leperos, & Indians, Franciscan missioneros & missiones, American & English commerciantes, puertos, presidios, castillos, sailors & backwoodsmen, revolutions & strife . . . . Reprinted from the first edition published in New York in 1846, and edited and corrected typographically with synopses of the chapters, and a foreword & notes . . . illustrated with reproductions, in mezzotint, direct from the litographs in the first edition. San Francisco, 1925.
>
> xxvii, 316 p., i l. front., illus., plates. 25½ cm.
>
> This volume does not contain the translation of Boscana's ''Chinigchinich'' which was appended to the first edition.

The Robinson volume was set in Caslon type, has head and tail pieces and a title page in red and black. According to Mrs. Barr, the paper is Duchess. The edition was of 250 copies.

> REZANOV, NIKOLAI PETROVICH. The Rezanov voyage to Nueva California in 1806, the report of Count Nikolai Petrovich Rezanov of his voyage to that provincia of Nueva Espana from New Archangel; an English translation revised and corrected, with notes etc. by Thomas C. Russell. Annotated, the County Rezanov: The Russian American company, the Krusenstern expedition, the settlements in Alaska—the Dona Concepcion Arguello: her family, her romantic and pathetic history—El Presidio de San Francisco, the historic, tragic, and alluring spot by the Golden Gate . . .

San Francisco, 1926.

 4 p. i., ix-xii, 104 p., i l. incl. facim. front. (port.) plates. 26 cm.

The paper of this edition of 260 copies was Strathmore. Head and tail pieces are lacking, but the red and black title page is again used. The type is Caslon.

 LANGSDORFF, GEORG HEINRICH. Langsdorff's Narrative of the Rezanov voyage to Nueva California in 1806, being that division of Dr. Georg H. von. Langsdorff's Bemerkungen auf einer reise um die Welt when, as personal physician, he accompanied Rezanov to Nueva California from Sitka, Alaska, and back; an English translation revised, with the Teutonisms of the original Hispaniolized, Russianized, or Anglicized . . . illustrated with portraits and a map. San Francisco, 1927.

 4 p. i., vii-xiv, 158 p., i l. front., plated (1 double) ports., fold. map, facsims. 26½ cm.

*Langsdorff's Narrative* was issued in an edition of 260 copies (to make it in number as well as content the companion piece of the *Rezanov*); the title page was black and red, the type Caslon, and the paper Antiquarian, according to Mrs. Barr. Again, tail and head pieces are lacking.

 SIMPSON, SIR GEORGE. . . . Narrative of a voyage to California ports in 1841-42, together with voyages to Sitka, the Sandwich Islands & Okhotsk, to which are added sketches of journeys across America, Asia & Europe. From the Narrative of a voyage around the world by Sir George Simpson . . . This edition edited, corrected typographically, with sketches of visits and journeys made outside of California, and with a foreword, new division synopses, and an ample index. . . . A facsimile reproduction of the original map in the London edition, enlarged reproduction of the signed last page of a report written by the author, two hand-printed photogravure protraits of the author, reproductions of the title-pages of the London and Philadelphia editions of 1847. San Francisco, 1930.

xxxii, 232 p. illus. (facsims.) 2 port. (incl. front.) fold. map. 26 cm.

This edition of 250 copies is described by Mrs. Barr as being on vellum-finished paper. The title page is in red and black. Initials opening the several divisions of the work are in red, and the usual Caslon type is employed.

It is upon these eight books, which Russell himself called "The Russell Reprints," that his reputation as a scholar and a printer was built. There can be little doubt that his reputation is as permanent as the quality of his workmanship.

The entire output of Reprints totalled 2,150 volumes; this is a remarkable production for a man who worked unaided, and who, by the beginning of the '20s, was already well advanced in years. It must also be remembered that Russell laid the scholarly basis for his Reprints himself. He was well known in the Bancroft Library, long before that collection was entirely catalogued, as a diligent and solitary researcher after the data that was later to appear in his finely edited books.

Entirely aside from the appearance of his printing, and the original subject matter he reprinted, Russell deserves great credit for the accuracy of his materials, for the care with which he prepared background material for the better understanding of the original texts, and for the remarkably fine indexes he supplied. He established, as well, a standard of spelling for those Spanish terms which had come into common usage among the English-speaking Californians, and was sufficiently sure of his editorship as to frankly assume all responsibility for his editorial efforts.

There are some who feel that the artistic level of Russell's work was not uniformly high. Taste in book esthetics, as in other areas, is a highly personal thing. In general, it can be said that while his works retain a flavor that is dated, they do so rightly in terms of their content. A fine printer is entitled to an occasional whim; Russell seems to have indulged in at least one whim when he used a Celtic metalwork motif in the head and tail pieces of the *Shirley Letters*. The designs are inherently attractive, but seem to strike a dissonant note in a work that was as American in subject and authorship as Mrs. Clappe's.

That Mr. Russell held a high opinion of his ability as an editor, proofreader, and printer is abundantly clear from his forewords. He had, by his own statement in Forbes' *California*, the "experience of a lifetime spent among printers, publishers, and authors" and he was quick to criticize the careless or ill-informed and poorly trained printer. The result is that he stands revealed by his own words as something less than kind toward those who first printed the books that he spent the last years of his life reprinting. However slipshod the work of those other printers whose presses brought forth the very works of Californiana that Russell recognized as so important, the fact remains that those works *were* published and *were* available for the instruction and enlightenment of thousands of persons long before Russell's day.

One would not wish to labor Russell's antipathy toward craftsmen less skilled and less scholarly than himself. The fact remains that whatever he may have thought of such men and their books, he saw an opportunity to reprint their works and give them a greater luster than had previously been the case. Students of Western history must stand forever in his debt for what he accomplished.

Russell called his workship The Private Press of Thomas C. Russell. His press was private only in the sense that it was wholly a one-man operation. He planned and executed each book on the assumption that there would be sufficient subscribers to make it worth his while.

Then as now, fine books, well printed and of scholarly content, produced in limited quantity for the select few, and produced by an individual whose heart as well as hands have gone into their production, are not cheap and they are never inexpensive. Russell's works ranged from $10.00 to $15.00 each upon publication, and bring considerably more than that today if they are in good conditon. Actually, Mr. Russell did not dispose of all of his copies, some of which were still in sheets at the time of his death. These were acquired by Mr. Newbegin and bound up for sale to the delight of collectors and students who had previously been unable to obtain copies.

In the preparation of these notes, it was hoped that more facts concerning Mr. Russell might be discovered. The search, though not exhaustive, has failed to produce much that has not been previously reported. Mrs. Barr visited the Russell Press, but it is not clear that she met Mr. Russell. She made no mention of either *The California Reprint* or *Panoramic San Francisco, 1877*. Will Ransom in his *Private Presses* stated that "there is Thomas C. Russell in San Francisco, too modest or too diffident to cry his own wares, but who has some very good books to his credit relating to California and the West." Ransom did not list the *McGowan*, and omitted mention of the two earlier works.

That Mr. Russell was diffident or shy may well have been the case; certainly he was not a joiner. At no time was he a member of the California Historical Society, nor does his name appear on the rosters of the better known book clubs of the San Francisco area.

Most strange of all, for a man of his acknowledged accomplishment in the world of printing, and in a city noted for and proud of its typographers, one might have expected to have found extensive notice of his death in the papers of his adopted city. The only abituary discovered, thus far, was in the San Francisco *Examiner* of September 28, 1931: "Russell—In this city, Sept. 25th., 1931 Thomas Chalmers Russell, Husband of Minnie Russell, and Father of Beatrice A. Russell and Constance R. Spiering."

# VOYAGE OF THE SONORA IN THE SECOND BUCARELI EXPEDITION

TO EXPLORE THE NORTHWEST COAST
SURVEY THE PORT OF SAN FRANCISCO
AND FOUND FRANCISCAN MISSIONS AND
A PRESIDIO AND PUEBLO AT THAT PORT

THE JOURNAL KEPT IN 1775 ON THE SONORA

*by*

DON FRANCISCO ANTONIO MOURELLE

THE SECOND PILOT OF THE FLEET
CONSTITUTING THE SEA DIVISION
OF THE EXPEDITION

TRANSLATED

*by*

THE HON. DAINES BARRINGTON

FROM THE ORIGINAL
SPANISH MANUSCRIPT

REPRINTED LINE FOR LINE AND PAGE FOR PAGE FROM BARRINGTON'S MISCELLANIES
PUBLISHED IN LONDON IN 1781

*with*

CONCISE NOTES SHOWING THE VOYAGES OF THE EARLIEST
EXPLORERS ON THE COAST, THE SEA AND LAND EXPEDITIONS OF
GÁLVEZ AND OF BUCARELI FOR SETTLING CALIFORNIA AND FOR
FOUNDING MISSIONS, AND MANY OTHER INTERESTING NOTES
AS WELL AS AN ENTIRELY NEW INDEX TO BOTH TEXT & NOTES

*by*

THOMAS C. RUSSELL

TOGETHER WITH A REPRODUCTION OF THE DE LA BODEGA SPANISH CARTA
GENERAL SHOWING SPANISH DISCOVERIES ETC. ON THE COAST UP TO 1791
AND ALSO A PORTRAIT OF SIR DAINES BARRINGTON

SAN FRANCISCO, CALIFORNIA
THOMAS C. RUSSELL
1734 NINETEENTH AVENUE
1920

# PUBLISHER'S FOREWORD

THE visitador general, José de Gálvez, at La Paz, in 1768, when providing, in "la santa expedición," for the establishing of Franciscan missions at San Diego and Monterey, was asked by Junípero Serra, "Nuestro Padre San Francisco, is he to have no mission?" To which Gálvez replied, "Let him show us his port, and he shall have a mission."

The port was shown, but in an unexpected way, in that expedition, in 1769. The founding of the mission was not accomplished so easily. Seven toilsome years were to pass before that was brought about in 1776. The struggles of that period are briefly recorded in this volume, in the text and notes.

The indefatigable Serra visited Bucareli in Mexico in 1773, and, among other matters, impressed upon that great Viceroy of Nueva España the necessity of protecting the Franciscan missions and the coasts of the Californias,—the Russians were threatening from the North, the English seeking a Northwest Passage,—and the advisability of founding more missions,—two at the new port of San Francisco. Serra also supported Anza in his proposed plan to establish an overland route from Sonora to the sea, and in the following year—1774—this was accomplished,—from Tubac in Sonora to Monterey in Nueva California. Serra returned to California with Pérez in the Santiago in 1774, and this voyage—the first Bucareli expedition—northward of California, in which nothing was accomplished, caused dissatisfaction both in Mexico and in Spain.

Now for the first time in the pages of history is perceived a definite combined plan for the exploration of and the establishment of fortified ports on the Northwest Coast, and for the establishment of a presidio, pueblo, and Franciscan missions at the new port of San Francisco,—the second Bucareli expedition. There is no evidence in the Journal of Mourelle of the far-reaching purposes of Bucareli in this expedition. The youthful but heroic piloto had but an eye single to his duties as a sailor, and to record faithfully in his Journal the happenings on this historic early voyage on the Californian and northwestern coasts. Although he records the endeavor to find the port of San Francisco, yet he, like other navigators of that time, confounds the old port with the new, and he does not state that the comandante of the fleet had orders to survey the new port. Thus, standing alone, the

Journal is unsatisfying; hence the publisher has, in this new edition, endeavored to set out, by means of the notes, what was accomplished by the various divisions of the expedition as planned by Bucareli. Included therein are biographies of the officers of the expedition, and also records of the vessels employed, with the names of their officers and chaplains, so far as authentic information was obtainable.

It may be proper here to give an outline of the combined plan of Bucareli for the expedition of 1775. The sea division consisting of the Santiago and La Sonora, under the command of Don Bruno Heceta, was to explore the coast northwest from the port of San Francisco, and, on the return from the north, survey that port. "It so happened" that the San Carlos, employed as a supply-ship, met with a mishap in the harbor of San Blas, and, following this, she was ordered to sail with the Santiago and La Sonora and survey the new port of San Francisco. Ayala, the comandante of the San Carlos, was also to assist Rivera y Moncada, comandante militar at Monterey, in the erection of buildings for the use of Anza's troops and pobladores from Sonora, who were expected to arrive before the completion of the survey. Padre Presidente Serra, at the Misión San Carlos Borromeo de Monterey, was to send padres with Indian servants and equipments for the founding of the missions. Anza, whose second expedition to the sea is considered the land division of the second Bucareli expedition, was to turn over his command to Rivera upon his arrival at Monterey and proceed to the new port, assist Ayala in the survey, and select the sites for the new establishments,—presidio, pueblo, and missions.

But Rivera could not go to San Francisco as planned, neither did Anza arrive as expected, nor did Heceta pass through the Golden Gate on his return. Thus San Francisco was not founded in 1775, nor were its military and mission establishments. Ayala, in the San Carlos, however, surveyed the new port without assistance,—the first commander of a sea-going vessel to pass through the Golden Gate. The next year saw the foundation of the new town. How this was at length brought about is succinctly stated in its proper place in the notes.

It was deemed advisable to include in the notes short accounts of the voyages on the coasts of the Californias, and of the ports discovered or visited, up to the year 1775, as all really led up to the settlement of Nueva (or Alta) California by the Spaniards. Not a little attention is paid to the original place-names, and their meanings too. How many San Franciscans know that the first European to set foot on the Farallones was Sir Francis Drake in 1579? Or that he gave them their first name,—the Islands of Saint James? Saint James,—Santiago,—the battle-cry of the Spaniards when charging the Moors. Those who think the old harbor of San Francisco was named in honor of Sir Francis Drake will perceive an exchange of compliments. Wherever the Journal, or the notes thereto by Sir Daines Barrington, called for amplification or explanation or correction, the best authorities were drawn upon for assistance in annotating. Where there was a conflict,—and this was only too common, in all conscience,—it is hoped that a correct decision was made. A mere glance at the notes will show the wide field covered.

Of all the works used for reference purposes in making the notes, not one was well indexed. Much that is valuable in such works is available only at the expense of patience and time. It is hoped that the index to this edition of Mourelle will prove satisfactory. It was thought that the entire work, that is, both the Journal and the notes, may prove a stimulus to wider reading and research, hence the index was made as comprehensive as possible. In order to avoid repetition or unnecessary indexing, the words "note on," followed by the page number, is frequently used in the entries of persons, places, etc. Altogether, simplicity was the aim.

Sir Daines Barrington,* in his Preface to the Journal of Mourelle, adverts to the peculiar jealousy of the Spaniards with regard to their American dominions. They had reason to be jealous, and it would be interesting to know just how this precious Journal was obtained from the Spanish depósito. Once in England, its importance was recognized. Greenhow, in his History of Oregon and California (Boston, 1844), page 117, says of Barrington's Miscellanies (London, 1781), from which the Journal is here reprinted, that it is a rare book, and that the translation attracted much attention at the time of its appearance, and from it, and the short account given in the introduction to the Journal of Galiano and Valdés, all the information respecting the voyage has been hitherto obtained; and the notices of this expedition, relative to the Northwest Coast, are, for the most part, taken directly, or at second hand, from the abstracts of the Journal given by Fleurieu in his introduction to La Pérouse, and his introduction to the Journal of Marchand, both of which are filled with errors.

The entire text of the Journal, with the notes of Sir Daines Barrington, is, in this edition, reprinted line for line and page for page, without any changes, except the substitution of the short "s" for the long "f." The running-titles in this edition are an addition, and are an adaptation from the fly-leaf half-title of the Journal as printed in Barrington's Miscellanies. The original work carried no running-titles, and the folios were bracketed and centered at the top of the page; as, [46]. A reprint edition of the Journal was also published, evidently printed after the forms of the Miscellanies were worked off, and before they were taken off the press, the folios being changed, as well as the signatures, on the press. The folios and the signatures of both are reprinted in this edition. There was no title-page to the reprint, the fly-leaf half-title (page 1, *post)* serving the purpose. This edition is repaged throughout, regularly. It may properly be said here that the head and tail pieces embellishing this edition are new designs, and specially engraved for

---

* Sir Daines Barrington was born in 1727 and died in 1800. He was the fourth son of John Shute, the first Viscount Barrington, said to be descended from Robert Shute, a judge in the reign of Queen Elizabeth. The family name was changed to Barrington by royal license. Sir Daines was an English polyglot lawyer, but he never got to be any higher than a Welsh judge. He possessed a versatile mind, and was the friend of Bishop Percy, Johnson, Boswell, and other literary men of his time. In 1768 he conversed with Dolly Pentreath, the last person who could speak Cornish. This woman died in 1788, aged 102.

that purpose.   No ornaments were used in the original edition of the Journal of Mourelle.*   The blank spaces over division-heads were relieved by parallel lines.

* Don Francisco Antonio Mourelle was born in San Adrián de Corme, Coruña, June 21, 1755, the scion of a noble family, then in reduced circumstances, whose family estate was called La Casa y Torre de Mourelle (= the House and Tower of Mourelle), situate in the jurisdicción of Jallas, Coruña.   The family name, — Mourelle, — which is said to be derived from the estate, is inaccurately spelled — Maurelle — in the Journal; but this error is found in other Spanish and foreign works, as well as such forms as Maurello, Maurell, Maurel, Morel, Mourelle de la Rua.   Don Francisco Antonio, in 1768, when thirteen years of age, entered the Spanish armada as a pilotín, or apprentice piloto.   He could not have served ten years in the Bay of Biscay, as stated by Sir Daines Barrington on page 8, post, as he was not twenty, and had served in the armada only seven years, when he was appointed segundo piloto of La Sonora in 1775.   His energy, devotion to duty, and tenacity of purpose, not to say heroism, without any indication of boastfulness, are everywhere apparent in the Journal; yet his youthful lack of vision is also apparent.   The San Carlos, lying in the harbor of San Blas with the Santiago and La Sonora, simply, to him, "so happened" to be there, and was "to proceed to the establishment at Monterey."   No importa nada.   And the new Puerto de San Francisco, discovered in 1769, which the comandante of his division had orders to survey, was, to him, the puerto of that name mentioned by Venegas.   But older heads than that of Mourelle were not a whit wiser.   In recognition of his services in 1775, Mourelle was, in 1776, promoted alférez de fragata.   In the third Bucareli expedition of 1779, he was segundo capitán of La Favorita, under De la Bodega, as stated in the note on page 90, post, and in 1780 was promoted alférez de navío. He was also highly commended in the naval records as "sobresaliente en pilotaje y maniobra táctica, disciplina, pertrechos y ordenanza, valor acreditado, con mucho talento y celo, buena conducta, nervio y entereza en el servicio."   In 1780–81 he sailed from Lisirán de Luzón to San Blas de California, discovering the Archipiélago Vavao (in the Friendly group), and other islands in the Pacific.   This voyage resulted in the work enritled Noticia de la navegación de la fragata Princesa al mando del alférez de fragata D. F. Mourelle desde Manila á San Blas por el océano Pacifico en 1780 y 1781. This work is in the Memorias del Depósito Hidrográfico, Madrid, and was, in part, published by Don Ricardo Beltrán y Rózpide in his La Polinesia (1884), and also in the Voyage of La Pérouse.   In the year 1787, Maurelle was promoted teniente de fragata and entered the cuerpo general de la armada.   Going to the City of México, he served from 1790 to 1793 as the secretary of the Viceroy of Nueva España, Don Juan Vicente Gúemez Pacheco de Padilla Horcasitas, Conde de Revillagigedo.   Here he was active in redeeming the city from its filth and brigandage.   Promoted teniente de navío, he returned to Spain, and, up to the time of his death in 1820, distinguished himself in the wars of that stirring period.   In 1799 he was promoted capitán de fragata, and served at the naval station of Algeciras, and in 1802 he was transferred to the naval station of Cádiz.   He was chief (= jefe) of the Algeciras station from December, 1804, until February, 1806, in the latter year being promoted capitán de navío, and given command of the naval station of Málaga.   In 1806 he was transferred to the more important naval station of Ceuta, opposite Gibraltar, and while here greatly distinguished himself in active service.   In 1809 he was made a member of the Junta de Defensa of Cádiz, and commander of the light forces of the port. In that year he went to Vera Cruz and Havana, returning in 1810 with treasure.   From 1810 to 1813 he was at Cádiz, assisting in the defense of the port, being in 1811 promoted brigadier (= commodore), made a member of the Consejo de Generales (= Council of Generals) in Puerto de Santa María (Cádiz), a knight of the Orden Militar de Santiago, and also received the grand cross of San Hermenegildo.   In November, 1818, he was appointed chief of the naval squadron which was to escort the troops to be sent to suppress the insurrection at Buenos

 # Northward *of* California *in* 1775

The Carta General of De la Bodega, the comandante of La Sonora, has been reproduced and inserted in this edition.   Showing as it does the old Spanish place-names from Puerto de Acapulco to the Aleutian Islands, it should, in connection with the notes* sent to Madrid with the original draft, which was made at San Blas,

Aires.   On January 1, 1820, when the fleet was about to sail, the popular insurrection of Rafael del Riego y Núñez broke out, and Mourelle, who was not in sympathy with the revolutionists, attacked and defeated them at the island of Cádiz.   The King (Fernando VII), however, consented to the proposed new constitution, and Mourelle gave him his support in March, 1820.   This insurrection caused the dissolution of the expedition to Buenos Aires, and Mourelle surrendered his command on April 18th. After several disappointments, caused by the new political situation, he died in Cádiz, May 24, 1820.

*The notes referred to above are translated rather freely into English and printed here.   A few explanatory facts are bracketed.

Sebastián Vizcaíno surveyed the coast from Acapulco to 43° N. in 1603.

El Golfo de California, or Mar de Cortés, was surveyed by Padre Consaga in 1745.

El Cabo Mendozino was discovered at the time Don Antonio de Mendoza was viceroy of Nueva España [1535–1549].

El Puerto de San Francisco was discovered and surveyed by Don Juan Manuel de Ayala in 1775, although knowledge was had of this port before that time, but it was not the same [port as that previously known; that is, it was not the Puerto de San Francisco of Cermeño.   As to its discovery in 1769, see page 103, post.]

El Puerto de la Bodega was discovered and entered in 1775 by Don Juan Francisco de la Bodega y Quadra.

El Puerto de la [Santísima] Trinidad was discovered, surveyed, and taken possession of in 1775 by Don Bruno Hezeta and Don Juan Francisco de la Bodega.

La Entrada de Hezeta [the mouth of the Columbia River] was seen from a long distance by Don Bruno Hezeta in 1775; and although it has not so far been surveyed, yet we are considering doing so this year.

La Ensenada de los Mártires was discovered in 1775 by Don Juan Francisco de la Bodega y

Quadra, who so named it because seven of his men were killed there by the Indians.

El Estrecho [= strait] de Fuca, it is said, was discovered in 1692; and although surveyed and taken possession of in 1789 and 1790 by Don José de Narvaez and Don Manuel Quimper, yet one mouth [= voca] has not yet been inspected, but it is purposed to do so this year.

El Puerto de Nuca [Nootka Sound] is the same name as that applied by the natives.   In La Punta de San Estevan, to the south, Don Juan Pérez anchored in 1774 [in the first Bucareli expedition].   Cook, after this, [in 1778,] surveyed the puerto, naming it King George['s Sound]; but in 1789 Don Estevan Martinez took possession and erected an establishment, whereupon the place was named San Lorenzo. We have now only to determine whether the place is an island, as some think it is; this, however, may have already been determined, as orders were given to survey it.

La Entrada de Don Juan Pérez ó de Font, although not yet explored, was seen by Pérez in 1774, and, according to the report of the voyage of Font, which is regarded as chimerical, was discovered in 1640; but we will determine the matter this year.

El Puerto de Bucarely was discovered, surveyed, and taken possession of by Don Juan Francisco de la Bodega y Quadra in 1775, but its extent prevented a complete survey.   This puerto is considered of such importance, not only on account of its size, but also because of the number of its inhabitants, that orders were issued to reconnoiter it this year.

La Ensenada del Príncipe, La Ensenada del Susto, Cabo de [del] Engaño, Puerto de Guadalupe, and La Isla de Lobos were discovered and reconnoitered by Don Juan Francisco de la Bodega y Quadra in 1775.

El Puerto de los Remedios was discovered, surveyed, and taken possession of in 1775 by Don Juan Francisco de la Bodega y Quadra. The natives were few, but warlike, and placed on the banks of a river teeming with fish.

prove of more than passing interest to the reader and the student of history. The Plano del Puerto de San Francisco of Ayala (the original survey of the new port of San Francisco in 1775) is also reproduced, and is added to the Carta. The Plano, with its old Spanish names of places around the bay, in connection with the note on San Francisco (post, pages 103 et seq.) should prove equally interesting with the Carta General, of which it is now a part. The one-page map added to the Journal on its first publication, is also printed in this new edition.

Although the publisher of this edition of the Journal of Mourelle has personally performed all the letterpress of the work,—that is, typesetting, proof-reading, and presswork,—and also compiled the notes and made the index, yet he desires to express his acknowledgment of much assistance rendered when gathering original information, or when struggling to settle the questionable or disputed points which were ever presenting themselves. Such acknowledgment is especially due to Dr. Herbert I. Priestley of the Academy of Pacific Coast History, Berkeley. Captain Henry Taylor, principal of Taylor's Nautical Academy, San Francisco, cleared up many questionable nautical facts found in the histories. Captain Harry W. Rhodes of the United States Lighthouse Board was generous in rendering assistance, as also were Captain Edmund F. Dickins and Fremont Morse of the Coast and Geodetic Survey. Mr. Robert Ray, librarian of the Public Library, deserves special mention. To that fine old San Francisco pressman, James E. Benson, a youthful pioneer of San Francisco, and the son of a pioneer, many thanks are due. It is to be regretted that whole-hearted acknowledgment cannot be tendered the many authors consulted in compiling the notes to this work. It so happened that some of the most useful works were printed in nondescript or job-printing offices. The strict discipline of a book-printing office is unknown in such places, nor is a proof-reader tolerated, and it is impossible for any author to emerge with credit. Many well-printed works were almost useless by reason of either a poor index or none. In any case, thanks are due to each and all for what proved to be of any assistance.

SAN FRANCISCO, July, 1920.                                    THOMAS C. RUSSELL.

El Cabo de San Elías, La Montaña de San Elías, La Isla del Carmen, La Ensenada de Valdés, and El Puerto de Santiago in La Isla de la Magdalena, were discovered in 1779 by Don Ignacio Arteaga and Don Francisco de la Bodega y Quadra, in which voyage [the third Bucareli expedition] possession was taken at [El Puerto de] Santiago, survey made of Las Bocas de Quadra, and also of La Isla de Quirós, now called [Isla] de Montague.

Las Islas de Regla, which lie at La Entrada de la Rivera de Cook, were discovered and taken possession of in 1779 by Don Ignacio Arteaga and Don Juan Francisco de la Bodega y Quadra. In that year, also, the Volcan de Miranda, and several other islands, were discovered.

The two Russian establishments in La Isla Cadiac and [La Isla de] Onalasca were examined in 1788 by Don Estevan Martínez and Don Gonzalo de Haro, who took possession thereof, and of La Isla de [la Santísima] Trinidad.

In 1790, Don Salvador Fidalgo resurveyed La Ensenada de Valdés, traded with the Russians at the establishments on La Rivera de Cook and on La Isla Cadiac, but none of the five which they now possess are worthy of consideration, although they may become respectable in the future, because of the system of government.

LIST OF PUBLICATIONS

Known printings of Don Francisco Antonio Mourelle including material in several printings of La Perouse.

*Abstract of a Narrative of an Interesting Voyage from Manilla to San Blaz in 1781 and 1782.* (In La Perouse, J.F.D.de. A Voyage Round the World, 1801, pp. 259-290.)

*Extract From the Narrative of a Voyage Made in 1779 by Don Francisco-Antonio Mourelle, Ensign of a Frigate, in the Service of the King of Spain, for Discovering the West Coast of North America.* 21 p., 21 cm., In "La Perouse," J.F. de G., A Voyage Round the World. p. 418-439.

*Journal of a Voyage in 1775. To explore the coast of America, northward of California. By the second pilot of the fleet, Don Francisco Antonio Mourelle, in king's schooner, called the Sonora, and commanded by Don Juan Francisco de la Bodega.* London, 1780(?) Tr. from the Spanish.

*Journal of a Voyage in 1775. To explore the coast of America, northward of California by . . . Francisco Antonio Mourelle.* In Barrington, Daines, Miscellanies, London, 1781, p. 471-477, 471-435, chart).

*Narrative of an interesting voyage in the frigate la Princesa from Manilla to San Blaz, in 1780, and 1781.* In Laperouse, J.F. de G., comte de. A voyage round the world . . . London, 1798. 22 cm. v. 1. p. 340-418. fold. map.

*Laperouse, Jean Francois de Galaup, comte de, 1741-1788. Voyage de la Perouse autour du monde, publie conformement au decret du 22 avril 1791, et redige par m. L.A. Millet-Mureau* . . . Paris, Imprimerie de la Republique, an. v. 1797.

*Voyage of the Sonora in the second Bucareli expedition to explore the Northwest coast, survey of the port of San Francisco, and found Franciscan missions and a presidio and a pueblo at that port; the journal kept in 1775 on the Sonora, by Don Francisco Antonio Mourelle, the second pilot of the fleet constituting the sea division of the expedition*; tr. by the Hon. Daines Barrington from the original Spanish manuscript; reprinted line for line and page for page from Barrington's Miscellanies published in London in 1781, with concise notes showing the voyages of the earliest explorers on the coast, the sea and land expeditions of Galvez and of Bucareli for settling California and for founding missions, and many other interesting notes as well as an entirely new index to both text & notes, by Thomas C. Russell; together with a reproduction of the de la Bodega Spanish Carta general showing Spanish discoveries, etc., on the coast up to 1791 and also a portrait of Sir Daines Barrington. San Francisco, Calif., T.C. Russell, 1920.

*A voyage round the world, performed in the years 1785, 1786, 1787, 1788, by M. de la Peyrouse*: abridged from the original French journal of M. de la Peyrouse, which was lately published by M. Milet-Mureau, in obedience to an order from the French government. To which are added, a voyage from Manilla to California, by Don Antonio Mourelle: and an abstract of the Voyage and discoveries of the late Capt. G. Vancouver. Boston, Printed for Joseph Bumstead, Sold by him at no. 20, Union-Street: by Thomas and Andrews, Newbury-Street; by E. and S. Larkin, Wm. P. and L. Blake, W. Pelham, and C. Bingham, Cornhill, 1801.



XXV

# The Russell California Volumes

ALL IN LIMITED, NUMBERED, REGISTERED EDITIONS — ALL TYPOGRAPHY DONE BY HAND
SOLD ONLY BY SUBSCRIPTION — CIRCULARS UPON APPLICATION
PRICES NOT GUARANTEED

## California. A History of Upper and Lower California from their First Discovery to the Present Time [1835]

¶ Comprising an Account of the Climate, Soil, Natural Productions, Agriculture, etc. A full View of the Missionary Establishments, and Condition of the Free and Domesticated Indians. With an Appendix relating to Steam-Navigation in the Pacific. With a New Map, Plans of the Harbors, and Numerous Engravings. By ALEXANDER FORBES, ESQ. London: 1839.

*** Reprinted in a limited edition of 250 copies, each copy numbered, signed, and registered. In this new edition all the original lithographed illustrations are reproduced and colored by hand; and the copper-engraved lithographed map is reproduced in the original six colors. A new index, a foreword, etc., are added. 1919.   [OUT OF PRINT]

### The Narrative of Edward McGowan

¶ Including a Full Account of the Author's Adventures and Perils while Persecuted by the San Francisco Vigilance Committee of 1856. Together with a Report of his Trial, which Resulted in his Acquittal. San Francisco: 1857.

*** Reprinted in a limited edition of 200 numbered and signed copies. All the old woodcuts in facsimile. 1917.                    [OUT OF PRINT]

## Voyage of the Sonora in the Second Bucareli Expedition

¶ To explore the Northwest Coast, Survey the Port of San Francisco, and Found Franciscan Missions and a Presidio and Pueblo at that Port. The Journal Kept in 1775 on the Sonora by DON FRANCISCO ANTONIO MOURELLE, the Second Pilot of the Fleet, and translated by the HON. DAINES BARRINGTON from the original Spanish MS. London: 1781.

*** Reprinted in a limited edition of 230 copies, numbered, signed, and registered. With many notes, showing the voyages of the earliest explorers on the coast, etc.; also a reproduction of the large Spanish carta general, showing the Spanish discoveries on the coast up to 1791, etc. 1920. Quarto. Price $15.00, net.

## The Shirley Letters from California Mines in 1851–52

¶ A Series of Letters from DAME SHIRLEY (MRS. LOUISE AMELIA KNAPP SMITH CLAPPE) to her Sister in Massachusetts. With Synopses of the Letters, a Foreword, and many Typographical and other Corrections and Emendations. Together with an Appreciation by Mrs. M. V. T. Lawrence.

*** Reprinted from the Pioneer Magazine of 1854–55, in a limited edition of 450 numbered, signed, and registered copies. Many fine hand-colored illustrations of early mining scenes. 1922. A handsome gift-book. Price $15.00, net.

### Life in California Before the Conquest

¶ Hispano-Californians, Léperos and Indians, Franciscan Misioneros and Misiones, American and English Comerciantes, Puertos, Presidios and Castillos, Sailors and Backwoodsmen, Revolutions and Strife. By ALFRED ROBINSON, an American Comerciante in the Mexican Territorio of Nueva California after 1829.

*** Reprinted from the first edition published in New York in 1846. Edited and corrected, with synopses of the chapters, and a foreword and notes. The illustrations in the first edition are reproduced in facsimile by the mezzotint process. A limited edition of 250 numbered, signed, and registered copies. Price $15.00, net.

## La Doña Concepción Argüello

LA BELLEZA DE LA NUEVA CALIFORNIA

*The Three Books Giving the Authentic Story of the Romance of Spanish California*

## The Rezanov Voyage to Nueva California in 1806

¶ The Report of COUNT NIKOLAI PETROVICH REZANOV of his Voyage to that Provincia of Nueva España from New Archangel, Alaska. An English Translation. Revised and Corrected. With Notes on Count Rezanov: The Russian American Company, The Krusenstern Expedition, The Settlements in Alaska – The Doña Concepción Argüello: Her Family, Her Romantic and Pathetic History – El Presidio de San Francisco, the Historic, Tragic, and Alluring Spot by the Golden Gate.

**** "The first footstep of a Russian on the soil of Nueva California." The MS. translation of the report in the Academy of Pacific Coast History at Berkeley, California, was diligently compared in following the original Russian in the History of the Russian American Company printed at Saint Petersburg. It was with no little satisfaction that this Press was enabled to present Rezanov as an honorable man. It is singular that the first translator failed in his duty to show that Rezanov was determined to carry out his nuptial vow with Doña Concepción. This duty done, historians would not have had an opportunity to express their doubts, nor would gushing sentimentalists have had their chance to win more tears over this reproach in the most appealing romance of Hispanic Nueva California. A limited edition of 260 numbered, signed, and registered copies. Illustrated. Price $15.00, net.

## Langsdorff's Narrative of the Rezanov Voyage to Nueva California in 1806

¶ Being that Division of DOCTOR GEORG H. VON LANGSDORFF's Bemerkungen auf einer Reise um die Welt, when, as Personal Physician, He Accompanied Rezanov to Nueva California from Sitka, Alaska, and Back. An English Translation. Revised, with the Teutonisms of the Original Hispaniolized, Russianized, or Anglicized.

**** Considered apart from his Narrative, Langsdorff is not an engaging character. He has been called "a thick-headed Hessian." No amount of persecution while in the Puerto de San Francisco could make him understand that he was an undesirable. His desertion of Rezanov at Sitka proves him a Hessian in one American sense, that is, a mere hireling, or one such ready to throw over a benefactor (which Rezanov was) for a better prospect or an immediate advantage. The present edition is limited to 260 numbered, signed, and registered copies, uniform in size with THE REZANOV VOYAGE. Many very fine illustrations, and a map showing the author's routes. Price $15.00, net.

## Sir George Simpson's Narrative of a Voyage to California Ports in 1841–42

¶ Together with Voyages to Sitka, the Sandwich Islands, and Okhotsk. To which are added Sketches of Journeys across America, Asia, and Europe. From the NARRATIVE OF A VOYAGE ROUND THE WORLD by SIR GEORGE SIMPSON, Governor-in-Chief of the Hudson's Bay Company's Territories in North America.

**** This edition has been edited and corrected, with sketches of visits and journeys made outside of California, and with a foreword, new synopses of the divisions, and an index, by Thomas C. Russell. A facsimile reproduction of the map in the London edition of 1847, and also reproductions of the title-pages of the London and Philadelphia editions. Two hand-printed photogravure portraits of the author. An enlarged reproduction of the signed last page of a report written by the author. A limited edition of 250 numbered, signed, and registered copies. Price $15.00, net.

*The* PRIVATE PRESS *of* THOMAS C. RUSSELL

1734 NINETEENTH AVENUE      SAN FRANCISCO, CALIFORNIA

*Descriptive Circulars sent upon application*

# ACCOUNT

## OF THE

# RUSSIAN DISCOVERIES

### BETWEEN

## ASIA AND AMERICA.

### TO WHICH ARE ADDED,

## THE CONQUEST OF SIBERIA,

### AND

## THE HISTORY OF THE TRANSACTIONS AND COMMERCE BETWEEN RUSSIA AND CHINA.

***

## By WILLIAM COXE, A. M.

Fellow of King's College, Cambridge, and Chaplain to his Grace the Duke of MARLBOROUGH.

***

LONDON,

PRINTED BY J. NICHOLS,

FOR T. CADELL, IN THE STRAND

MDCCLXXX.

# JOURNAL

*of*

# A VOYAGE IN 1775.

To Explore *the* Coast *of* America, Northward *of* California,

By *the* Second Pilot *of the* Fleet,
Don FRANCISCO ANTONIO MAURELLE,

In *the* King's Schooner, called *the* Sonora, *and* commanded *by*
Don JUAN FRANCISCO DE LA BODEGA.

# PREFACE.

THE following journal having been placed in my hands for perusal, I conceived it to be so interesting for the improvement of Geography, that I desired permission to translate and publish it.

I was principally induced to take this trouble, because I supposed, that the Spaniards, from their most peculiar jealousy with regard to their American dominions[a], would never permit that navigators of other countries (particularly the English) should know the excellent ports of the Western part of America in high Northern Latitudes, which are here laid down with such accuracy and precision, together with the abundant supply of masts, fire wood, and water which may be procured in most of them.

[a] That most able Historian Dr. Robertson, after having mentioned, that most of the American papers are deposited in the Archivo of Simanca, near Valladolid, thus proceeds :

"The prospect of such a treasure excited my most ardent curiosity ; "but the prospect of it only is all that I have enjoyed. Spain, with "an excess of caution, hath uniformly thrown a veil over her trans- "actions in America: from strangers they are concealed with peculiar "solicitude." Preface to the History of America, p. ix.

It

It appears, by Venegas's History of California, published in 1747[b], that great jealousy was then entertained of our discovering a N.W. passage[c], because they apprehended we should annoy the coasts of Mexico and Peru.

Nothing however can be more groundless than these suspicions, for whenever a N.W. or any other Northern communication is found between the Atlantic and Pacific Oceans, it may be boldly pronounced that such passage will be so very precarious, as never to answer the purpose of expeditions in time of war, or commerce during peace.

The Spaniards should, after our late voyages of discovery (which reflect so much honour upon his Majesty's reign), be convinced that the English Nation is actuated merely by desiring to know as much as possible with regard to the planet which we inhabit, and to which our geographical inquiries are necessarily bounded.

This distrust on the part of Spain would more wisely be directed against the Russians, who from Camskatska might easily establish themselves on the W. coast of America, and from thence perhaps in time shake their unwieldy, and already tottering empire[d].

From these ill-founded apprehensions of what the English may meditate against their American Dominions on the Western coast of that vast continent, they will not permit an individual,

[b] Madrid, 3 vol. Quarto.

[c] Igualmente notorias son las *ruidosas, y porfiadas* tentativas de los *Ingleses*, para hallar un passage al mar del *Sur,* por *el Norte de America.* Ibid. T. III. p. 225.

[d] I am accordingly informed, that the Empress means to fit out four vessels on the coast of Camskatska, which are to be employed in discoveries, during the proper season of 1781.

even

even of our nation, to set his foot in their part of America, even for scientific purposes[c].

Notwithstanding this perpetual distrust of this country in the Spaniards, and our present war with them, I will venture to say, that an attack upon the city or province of Mexico, would not be advisable on our part. If the Spaniards indeed acted wisely, they should themselves abandon it, for the mines

[c] The transaction I here allude to is the following. Lord Morton, as President of the Royal Society, applied to the then Spanish ambassador at our Court in 1766, for leave that an English Astronomer might observe the Transit of Venus (expected in 1769) on some part of California. This was however refused, when his Lordship requested, that Father Boscowich, a *foreigner* and *good Catholick*, might have the same permission; in which he was at first more successful, but the favour was even then granted with many clogs, and the permission at last recalled, on account of his being a Jesuit, who were at that time banished from Old and New Spain.

At the same time Chappe Dauteroche obtained this permission, and for the same purpose; the consequence of which hath been, that a draft of the city of Mexico, in its present state, was found amongst his papers, and published by his Catholic Majesty's good allies, the French, for the information of his enemies.

I once applied myself to the late Prince Masserano (so deservedly esteemed whilst resident as Minister of Spain in England) that an ingenious German, named Kukahn*, might be permitted, under any restrictions, to go from La Vera Cruz, to any part of the province of Mexico, merely to collect specimens of Natural History. I was also responsible that he never would attend to any thing, during his journies, but the animals he might meet with. Though I made this application by a channel which his excellency would have been desirous to oblige, yet he excused himself, from its being a fundamental rule with the Court of Spain, that no foreigner be permitted to pass through any part of their dominions on the continent of America.

* See an account of his method of preserving animals, and placing them in their proper attitudes. (Ph. Trans.) He is now established in Jamaica, and hath succeeded in raising many European fruits, as also products of our kitchen-gardens, in some ground which he hath purchased, about half way up a mountain.

within

within any convenient distance are nearly exhausted, whilst the charge of bringing quicksilver from La Vera Cruz is thereby greatly augmented. Venegas therefore informs us, that it is not worth while to work the more abundant mines of Sonora to the Northward, from this increase of expense. The silver indeed, at so distant a period as 150 years ago, was chiefly brought from St. Lewis de Sacatecas, which is nearly 100 leagues N. of Mexico[f]. This objection does not hold with regard to the continuing to work the silver mines of Peru, as the famous one of quicksilver, called *Guanacabelica*, is situated in the same province. It is believed also, that the *gold mines* in America, as they are improperly called, answer as little to the Spaniards. At least I have been informed, by a person who resided two or three years in Brasil, which furnishes the greatest quantity of this precious metal, that those who go in search of it are not paid above a shilling per day for their labours. Gold is never found in the state of ore, or by digging deep into the bowels of the earth; the adventurers therefore go in companies of five or six to explore those parts where they conceive themselves to have the best chance of finding it near the surface, but often return after being out months, with a very small portion, by which the fatigues and dangers they have incurred are poorly compensated.

As little would it answer to take possession of Acapulco, for the sake of an annual ship which would presently change its rendesvouz for another port, or of Panama, in order to inter-

---

[f] To this it may be added, that the situation of Mexico is very unhealthy, *Gage* comparing the many canals to those of Venice, which are often highly offensive. [See Gage's Survey of the W. Indies.] It is also subject to great inundations; and Don Alzate informs the Academy of Sciences at Paris, that during the years 1736 and 1768 more than one-third of the inhabitants died of the black vomit.

cept

cept the flotilla, which by late regulations is never to touch there[g].

The Spaniards moreover should learn from what England hath suffered by conquering Canada for our ungrateful colonies, that the settlement of a rival nation to the Northward of Mexico, would possibly operate in favour of the mother country.

We have experienced this most unnatural rebellion within a few years after we had removed the dread of the French in Canada from them, and after every fostering indulgence on our part. What may the Spaniards therefore have occasion to dread from their vast American Empire, the inhabitants of which they are perpetually oppressing with their enormous duties and taxes?

Thus much have I ventured to say in hopes that the court of Spain will rather promote, than obstruct, any future voyage of discovery, in the Northern parts of the Pacific Ocean.

I am sorry that I have not an opportunity of engraving with this journal the nine charts which should accompany it; but as the Latitudes and Longitudes of the new Discoveries on the coast of America are so accurately stated, I should hope that the publication will at least convince the Spaniards how little it will answer the purpose of mystery to withhold them.

It appears by this journal that the Viceroy of Mexico sent some other ships on discovery to the Northward in a preceding year, and

---

[g] The silver from Peru and Chili is either now sent over part of the Andes to Buenos Ayres, or otherwise transmitted in single register ships round Cape Horn. The establishment of Galeons sailing in a fleet from Cadiz being now also abolished, Carthagena, Porto Bello, and Panama, are become more than useless to the Spaniards, as the climates are bad, whilst the civil and military establishment at each is very expensive.

that

that they proceded to N. Lat. 55. Don Juan Peres, who was *ensign*[h] on board the Frigate in the present voyage, had some station in the former, and carried with him a chart of the coast, in many of the parts which were then explored.

I am sorry not to be able to state any further particulars, but think it right to mention thus much, in hopes that it may produce some account of this former voyage.

I should conceive, that both the one and the other were produced by our attempts to discover a N.W. Passage; because it will be found, that wherever the Spaniards landed they were instructed to take possession (though not to keep it) with every possible formality, which undoubtedly was to be set up as a complete title against future claimants, by right of discovery.

The compiler of the present journal, D. Antonio Maurelle, served on board the schooner employed on this voyage (together with a frigate) under the title of Second Pilot of the Fleet[i].

In one of the written opinions which he gave whilst thus employed, he states, that he had served ten years in the Bay of Biscay[k], and seems to have been a most diligent navigator; whilst, to his honour, he always advises the proceeding to as high a Northern Latitude as possible, though some of his brother officers almost despair.

At the close of the journal a very accurate table is given of the ship's course for each day, with no less than nine columns.

Having however consulted some most experienced and able sea-officers on this occasion, they have advised me only to print

[h] *Alferez.*

[i] I understand that we have no rank in our marine service which answers at all to this.

[k] The expression in the original is *Golfo de las Yeguas*, or the *Gulf of Mares*. The Spaniards also call the gulf of Mexico *Golfo de las Ciervas*, or Gulf *of Does*.

a few

a few of these heads[1], as some of them would not be easily understood by any navigator, who is not a Spaniard.

Upon the whole, it is hoped, that this account of an eight months navigation on the unfrequented coast of America, will prove a valuable addition to geography; especially as our immortal Captain Cook had so few opportunities of examining most parts of the same continent to the Westward[m], though his discoveries to the Northward will prove so interesting.

[1] It is right also to observe, that (though I give the column which states the Variation of the Needle) it is not specified whether the Variation is West or East; I should rather indeed suppose it to be the latter, on the authority of Dr. Halley, though perhaps the direction may have altered since the last century. This doubt however will be settled when Capt. Cook's last voyage is published.

[m] This is said to have been occasioned by unfavourable winds.

# PREFACE *of* DON ANTONIO MAURELLE.

FOR the better understanding this Journal, it will be proper to premise the following particulars.

The charts which we used during the voyage were those of Mons. Bellin, the one published in 1766, and the other in 17—; the first of which places the port of St. Blas, 110 degrees W. Long. from Paris, and the second 114, differing consequently 4 degrees.  For this reason I have always reckoned the Western Longitude from St. Blas[a], and not from Paris.

At the end there is an accurate table, every page of which includes a month, with an account of the Ship's course each day, together with the number of leagues sailed, the longitude, latitude, variation of the needle (which last, when attended to, is marked with an asterisk), and the distance from the nearest land.

---

[a] San Blas is a very small hamlet, on the W. coast of the province of Mexico, at the mouth of the River S. Pedro.  It is but within these few years that the Spaniards have made a settlement there, for the conveniency of transporting the troops and provisions they send to California. Dr. Robertson's map places it about the 22d degree of N. Lat. and 88th W. Long from Fero.  See also Chappe D'Auteroche's account of his journey from La Vera Cruz to S. Blas in 1769.  The Latitude of this port is not settled by this Journal, nor Longitude except by reference.



At

The plans of the ports which have been discovered, follow these tables, as also a chart of the whole coast, drawn with the greatest accuracy, as we always marked the most distinguishable points.  In order also that we might be more exact, we compared the ship's course with that of the coast, and repeated our observations, both in sailing Northwards, and returning to the South.

We likewise have omitted every longitude, in which we conceived there had been mistakes, by accidents that had happened, and when we only doubted in distances of no great moment, we have laid them down, making the proper allowances.

The latitudes of the charts[b] are marked with the greatest precision, in those situations where it may be of the most use, having had sufficient time to make the proper observations, whilst the allowances for refraction were attended to.

[b] These charts unfortunately did not accompany the Journal.

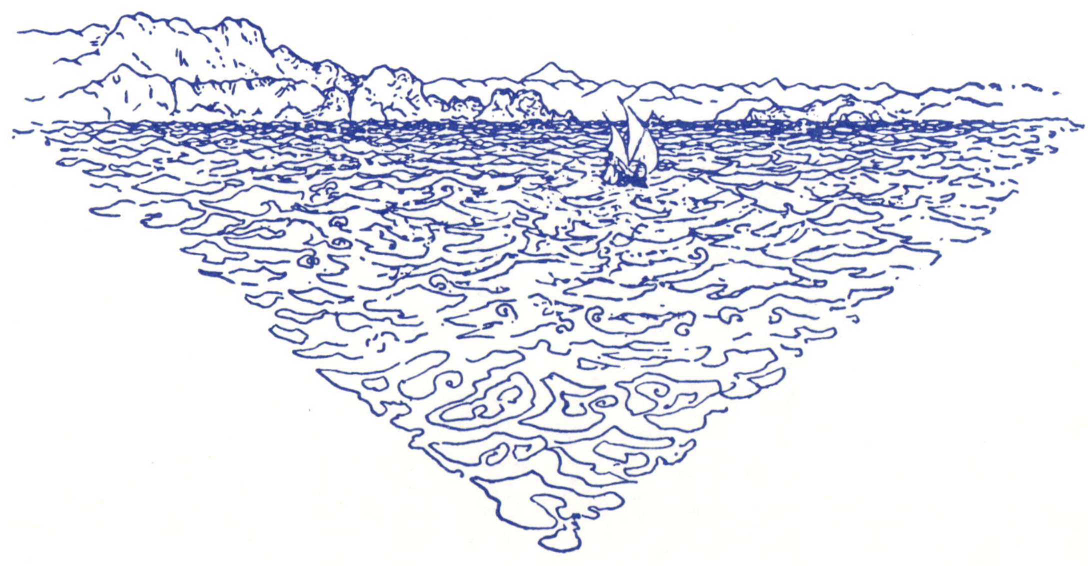

January, 1775.

BEING on board the King's storeship[c] the *Santa Rica,* which then lay in the port of Vera Cruz, I received on the 10th of that month an order from his Excellency the Viceroy[d] Don Antonio Maria de Bucarely and Orsua, to undertake the function of first pilot in the expedition, which was then fitting out at the port of St. Blas for discoveries on the Northern coast of California[e].

As I have always had the strongest desire to serve his Majesty (be the risque what it may) I readily accepted this commission, and setting out from La Vera Cruz on the 12th of January, I reached Mexico on the 18th in order to receive his Excellency's further commands. I left Mexico again on the 16th of February, and arrived at the Port of St. Blas[f], putting myself under the orders of the officer, who was to fit out the expedition, Don Bruno Heceta. The ships prepared for this purpose were a frigate and schooner[g], the latter being 36 feet long[h], 12 feet wide, and 8 deep, commanded by the Lieutenant Don Juan de Ayala, assisted by Don Juan Francisco de la Bodega, of the same

[c] Urca.

[d] Sc. of Mexico.

[e] It should seem from this journal, that the Spaniards deem all the N. W. coast of America beyond California to be part of that province.

[f] The journey from La Vera Cruz to Port S. Blas is supposed to be 300 leagues, thus divided : from La Vera Cruz to Mexico 110 leagues; and from the latter to S. Blas 190.

[g] Goleta.

[h] 18 codos, each codo being two feet.

rank,

rank, and I embarked in the schooner. It so happened that the pacquet-boat S. Carlos was at this time in the port of S. Blas, commanded by the Lieutenant D. Miguel Maurrique, who was to proceed to the establishment at Monterey[i].

Whilst we continued here, we laid in provisions for a year's voyage; all of which were procured from the neighbourhood.

On the 16th of March we had taken on board all such necessaries; and at 10 o'clock at night the three vessels set sail, steering N.W. with a gentle land-breeze at N.N.E. but though we did every thing in our power during the night to keep company with the other ships, we were not able, which we conceived to arise from the cargoe not being properly stowed, because the schooner's reputed rate of sailing, by those who were well-acquainted with her, left us scarcely any doubt with regard to this being the real cause.

As soon as day appeared on the 17th it grew calm, and continued so till three in the afternoon; when a breeze from the N.W. arising, we steered N.N.E. and towards the coast, till sun-set, when the wind fell. At this time we cast anchor, and found ourselves 4 leagues N.N.E. of S. Blas, and in this manner we prosecuted our voyage, making use of the sea-breeze during the day, and the land-breeze during the night, gaining very little to windward[k], and casting anchor when the wind fell, in order not to lose ground by the currents[l], after so little progress, and with such trouble.

---

[i] The latitude of Monterey is settled afterwards by this journal to be in 36 44 N. Lat. and 17 0 W. Long. from St. Blas. It is situated on the Western coast of California, and a mission of Jesuits is there established.

[k] Barlovento.

[l] The currents are so strong in this sea that a promontory S. of S. Blas is called Corrientes.

On

On the 13th at three in the evening the S. Carlos Pacquet-boat made a signal for help, on which our captain sent a boat, in which Don Mignel Maurique (who commanded the Pacquet) was brought to our ship, when we plainly discovered, by his actions, that he was out of his senses. On this our principal officers accompanied him on board the frigate, that the captain might give the proper orders on this occasion, when a council being held, and the surgeons examined, as well as ocular proofs appearing of D. Maurique's madness, it was determined to set him on shore, as also to give the command of the pacquet-boat to Don Juan d'Ayla, lieutenant of the frigate, and that of the schooner to Don Juan Francisco de la Bodega and Quadra, who had the same rank.

On the 20th, the breeze being moderate, it was discovered that the foretopsail[m] was rent in several places, which defect it was necessary to repair immediately.

Whilst the wind thus continued, the commander of the schooner tried many experiments, to make her sail better, one of which indeed rather improved her rate; but the frigate, notwithstanding, was still obliged to shorten sail, in order to keep us company, and indeed to take us in towe[n].

On the 24th at noon we had sight of the Southernmost of the Marias[o], lying to the N. E. at the distance of three leagues, which makes the then situation of our ship exactly a degree W. of S. Blas, according to M. Belin's map of 1756, and in N. Lat. 21. 4. m. Now this differs from my observations, being 26 minutes too far Northwards.

[m] El mastelero de velacho.

[n] In the original another experiment is stated, which I have not translated, as I conceive it would be uninteresting to the reader.

[o] There are three islands thus called.

Whilst

Whilst we were in this situation we lost sight of the pacquet-boat, but we continued our course steering S.W.[p] when we observed many birds, some of which were black, with a white spot on their breast, the wings long, beak rather large, belly prominent, and tail like a pair of scissars[q]; others again were entirely white; whilst some were grey, with a single large feather. We likewise saw other birds, which dived often under the water, named bobos.

During great part of March the wind freshened in the day, and fell at night, particularly a little before the new moon[r], (which happened on the 29th,) after which we had often calms, the wind having before blown from the N.W. to the N. on this same day (viz. the 29th) we saw an island at sunset, which is said to be called Socorro[s], by which name it is not to be found in the French maps, nor in the History of California[t]. We had a view of it whilst it lay to the Eastward at the distance of 9 or 10 leagues, which with difficulty we gained to windward[u], wishing to sail as nearly as possible upon the meridian of that island.

On the 30th we endeavoured to approach nearer to Socorro, when it lay W. N. W.[x] at the distance of four leagues, but

[p] Sudoeste quárta al oeste.

[q] Tixera.

[r] Great attention to the moon, and its supposed effects on the weather, is to be observed in other parts of this journal.

[s] This island, in Dr. Robertson's map, is placed in 19 N. Lat. and 94 W. Long. from Fero.

[t] This is probably the history of that country published by Miguel Venegas (a Mexican Jesuit) at Madrid, in 1758, which was translated into English, and printed at London in 1759. It is not at all extraordinary however that this island should not be mentioned in that account, as Venegas chiefly describes the E. coast of California. Socorro is considerably to the South of that Peninsula.

[u] Orzando.

[x] Quarta al oeste.

we

we could not effect this on account of the currents to the S. which carried us to Leeward [y].

From the 31st of March till the 4th of April we had either calms or light breezes, on which account we could not sail further from this island than we lost by the currents.   For this reason also we tried by towing the schooner, and using of our oars, whether we might not make some part of the island, where we might procure water; but in this we could not succeed on account of the violent currents.

This island, which, as was said before, is not named Socorro in any maps, is undoubtedly that which was discovered by Hernando Triabba, who commanded a ship dispatched from Guantepeque, by Hernan Cortes, to explore the coast of California. This vessel sailed 300 leagues ————— [z] and fell in with an island named St. Thomas, which is so called in the French maps, though erroneously placed, because its real latitude is 18° 53′ N. Lat. and W. Long. from S. Blas 5° 18′.

On the 4th of April we lost sight of Socorro to the E. N. E. and prosecuted our voyage to windward as much as possible, without any other accident but the frigate's bowsprit being damaged, which we soon repaired.

At this time we found that the sky was not so clear as before, we approached Socorro, that the sun did not appear so frequently, that the mists were not so thick, that the wind was much more cold, and in short we experienced a very different temperature.

Till the 14th, when the full moon happened, the breezes were slight, and the currents always to the South, after this

[y] Sotovento.

[z] There is a chasm in the MS with regard to the direction in which she sailed.

however

however the wind freshened to the N. N. E. sometimes flitting to the N. E. and blowng more strongly from that point. By these means we had an opportunity of trying the sailing capacity of the schooner, for the rougher the sea the more sail was set, so that the deck was constantly two planks* under water to leeward; which thoroughly convinced those on board the frigate of our determined resolution to prosecute our voyage.

The crews of both ships, who observed what a press of sail was carried by the schooner, from the determined resolution of the officers to proceed as far Northward as possible, saw plainly that they were in some degree mistaken, by conceiving at our first departure that the schooner would be obliged to return to S. Blas in a fortnight. They however still shewed their apprehensions if she pursued her voyage, whilst some of the schooner's company began to sicken, and wish themselves on board the frigate, where there were medicines and a surgeon. The surgeon however declared, that if such seamen were removed to the frigate, they would be probably seized with a fever, on which the Captain thought it right that this opinion should be made known to the schooner's crew, as he supposed it would have a greater effect than the threats of any punishment. To say the truth, we could not but be sorry to observe the horror that the crew conceived of the bad condition of the schooner, which afforded miserable quarters for the sick, as the seamen could not do the business without being thoroughly wet, except when it was calm.

These distresses would have become insufferable, had not the commander behaved with the greatest kindness to the crew, he encouraged them to persist also, by giving them frequently small

presents,

presents, and reminded them of the glory they would obtain on their return, if they reached the proper latitude[b]. He added also, that the risque was nearly equal[c] to both vessels, and that as each ship's company valued their lives, they might be sure that it would not be attempted to proceed further than was consistent with their mutual safety. This interposition of the commander had at length the proper effect, and we agreed to live and dye together.

On the 11th of May the wind began to veer about, and on every point to the Eastward, but ended to the E. & S. E. with many squalls[d] and mists. The strong currents which we had before experienced to the S. were now scarcely to be perceived.

On the 21st our commander held a council, in which it was to be determined whether we should continue our voyage, or put into the establishment at Monterey, and that the resolutions we should come to might be the more deliberate, our opinions, with the reasons on which they were founded, were reduced to writing. As the wind however was very violent, there could be no personal communication between the officers of the two ships, and our opinions were therefore transmitted by means of a cask.

[These opinions follow, in the journal at length, but as they would not be very interesting even to the navigator, I shall only state that they all agree in advising that they should proceed as far N. as 43. rather than put into Monterey. The principal

[b] It appears afterwards that they were instructed to proceed as far N. as 65 if practicable.

[c] It must be recollected that at this time the frigate towed the schooner.

[d] Chuvascos, which is supposed to be a term used in the Mexican Seas.

reason

reason for this advice is, that Martin de Aguilar had discovered a river in this latitude, where they hoped consequently to water, and repair their vessels[e].]

We proceeded on our voyage therefore with brisk winds from the N. & N.N.E. the sea running high till the 30th, when the new moon happened during which interval we made many tacks, and did not accurately observe our longitude or latitude.

On this same day we had gentle breezes between N.W. & S.W. varying thus for the three following days, after which the wind was steady in the W.N.W. and blew fresher as the moon increased.

On the first of June one of our seamen was so drunk with spirits that we thought it right to remove him to the frigate[f], where he afterwards died in less than six hours. On the same day we observed some sea-weeds, the top of which much resembled an orange[g], from the upper part of which hung large and broad leaves.

At the extremity of this plant is a very long tube, which fixes to the rocks on the coast till it is loosened by the sea, when it often floats to the distance of 100 leagues. We named this plant the *Orange-head.*

The next day we saw another plant, with long and narrow leaves like a ribband, which is called *Zacate del Mar*; we also saw many sea-wolves, ducks, and fish.

[e] In the account of this voyage in 1601, added to Venegas's History of California, this river is said to have been discovered by the pilot Lopes, and not by Martin de Aguilar. In some maps it is placed in 45 N. Lat.

[f] Because there was a surgeon on board that ship, probably.

[g] Una naranja.

On the 5th our towing rope[h] was broke; which indeed had happened several times before, notwithstanding the greatest care of both ship's companies, on which accident we resolved to proceed, as well as we could, without this very inconvenient appendage.

On the 7th, from the colour of the sea, we judged ourselves to be in soundings, and we supposed ourselves to be about thirty leagues from the coast.

By noon on the same day we distinguished a large tract of the coast (though at a considerable distance) lying from the S.W. to the N. E. but we were not able to get nearer to it, by the winds falling calm during the night and the following day.

On the 8th we saw the coast much clearer at the distance of about 9 leagues, and the next 24 hours the currents to the S. increased strongly, so that there was a difference in the latitude by observation and our reckoning of 29 minutes.

The same day the wind freshening, the commander made signal for the schooner to reconnoitre the coast, which direction we complied with to our utmost, steering to the N. N. E. and. hoping to do this before the night. In effect, by six in the evening, we distinguished many headlands, bays, plains, and mountains, with trees and green fields.

By eight at night we were not more than two leagues distant from the land, nor the frigate more than three; we then sailed towards her, and thus passed the night.

On the 9th at break of day the frigate made us a signal to join them, and by 10 in the morning we followed their course till we came to another part of the coast, where we saw, with the greatest clearness, the plains, rocks, bays, headlands, breakers,

and

and trees: here we sounded in 30 fathoms, the bottom being a black sand. At the same time we sailed along the coast, and endeavoured to find out a port, being at the distance only of a mile, and approaching to a high cape, which seemed to promise shelter, though we were obliged to proceed cautiously, as many small islands concealed from us some rocks, which scarcely appeared above the surface of the sea.

As we now perceived a land-locked harbour to the S.W. we determined to enter it, making at the same time a signal to the frigate to lend us an anchor, which however they were not able to do, from their distance, as well as that the wind blew fresh. For these reasons the schooner entered the port alone, sounding all the way, with the greatest care, and the frigate followed in our wake.

Whilst we were thus entering the port, we observed two canoes from the N. which came close to the frigate, and exchanged their skins for bugles, and other trifles, with our seamen, whilst in the mean time the schooner cast anchor opposite to a little village[k], which was situated at the bottom of a mountain: the inhabitants however did not send out any canoes to us.

After this we sounded the interior parts of the port, and we found sufficient depth of water to anchor at a bow's shot from the land, we saw likewise the frigate at the bottom of the port, and fastened our cables to some rocks which nature seemed to have fixed there for this purpose. We took however the precaution to let fall two anchors on the opposite side; (viz. to the S. and S.W.) on which the frigate followed our example.

As

As soon as we had anchored, some Indians in canoes came on board, who, without the least shyness, trucked some skins for bugles.

And here it may be right to observe the inaccuracies of the French map[1], both with regard to the capes, and the lying of the coast. It should seem indeed that the absolute want of authentic materials hath been the occasion of laying down at random some large bays, which we neither found to the N. or to the S. as we must certainly have fallen in with them above Cape Fortuna, which is placed 18 leagues to the S. of Cape Mendocino[m], whereas we were twenty leagues to the N. which makes an error of two degrees of latitude[n].

On the 11th we had fixed every thing with regard to our anchorage, and we determined to take possession of the country, upon the top of a high mountain, which lyes at the entrance of the port. For this purpose our crews divided into different parties, which were properly posted, so that the rest might proceed without any danger of an attack. We moreover placed centinels at a considerable distance, to reconnoitre the paths used by the Indians, who possessed themselves of those parts from which we had most to fear. With these precautions the crews marched in two bodies, who adored the holy cross upon disembarking, and when at the top of the mountain formed a square, the centre of which became a chapel. Here the holy cross was again raised, mass celebrated, with a sermon, and possession taken, with all the requisites enjoined by our instructions. We also fired both

[1] Of Mons. Bellin.

[m] So called from Mendoza, a Viceroy of Mexico, who sent some ships on discovery. Most maps place this on the N. W. point of California.

[n] De ocho cavos.

our

our musquetry and cannon, which naturally made the Indians suppose we were irresistible.  After they had recovered their fright however, and found that we had done them no harm, they visited us again, and probably to examine more nearly what had occasioned the tremendous noise which they had never heard before.  As we thus took possession on the day when holy mother church celebrates the festival of the most holy Trinity, we named the port accordingly°.

The following days were taken up in procuring wood and water, whilst the schooner was careened.  We likewise cut some masts for her.

We could not but particularly attend to all the actions of the Indians, their manner of living, habitations, garments, food, government, laws, language, and arms, as also their[p] hunting and fisheries.  The distrust indeed which we naturally entertained of these barbarians, made us endeavour to get as great an insight into all these as possible, yet we never observed any thing contrary to the most perfect friendship and confidence which they seemed to repose in us.  I may add, that their intercourse with us was not only kind, but affectionate.

There houses were square, and built with large beams, the roofs being no higher than the surface of the ground, for the

---

° There is certainly some use to geographers in this custom of the Spaniards naming places from the Saint's day in which they take possession, or make the discovery, as it points out to posterity the time of the year when the event happened.

[p] Sus *cazas*, which like the French word *chasse* and Italian *caccia*, comprehends also fowling.  In Sir Ashton Lever's most capital museum may be seen what contrivances are used by the Indians of St. George's Sound N. Lat. 50. on this same coast and for these purposes.  There is also in the same noble repository some birdlime from the newly discovered Sandwich islands.

doors

doors to which they make use of a circular hole, just large enough for their bodies to pass through. The floors of these huts are perfectly smooth and clean, with a square hole[q] two feet deep in the centre, in which they make their fire, and round which they are continually warming themselves, on account of the great cold. Such habitations also secure them, when not employed out of doors, from the wind and noxious animals.

The men however do not wear any covering, except the cold is intense, when indeed they put upon their shoulders the skins of sea-wolves, otters, deer, or other animals: many of them also have round their heads[r] sweet-smelling herbs. They likewise wear their hair either dishevelled over their shoulders, or otherwise *en castanna*[s].

In the flaps of their ears they have rings like those at the end of a musquet[t].

They bind their loins and legs quite down to the ancles, very closely, with strips of hide or thread.

They paint their face, and greater part of their body, regularly either with a black or blue[u] colour.

Their arms are covered with circles of small points in the same manner that common people in Spain often paint ships and anchors.

[q] Oyo or eye literally.

[r] Una rueda, literally a garland in the form of a wheel.

[s] The Spaniards apply castanna to a particular method of dressing the hair — *peinado en castanna*, literally signifies, hair dressed to resemble a chesnut tree.

[t] I am informed by a gentleman long resident in Spain, that it is not unusual to have rings so placed, and that they are of use to prevent the knapsack from falling off.

[u] Azarcon.

The

The women cover the tops of their heads with an ornament like the crest of a helmet[x], and wear their hair in two tresses[y], in which they stick many sweet-smelling herbs. They also use the same rings in their caps (which are of bone) as the men are before described to do, and cover their bodies with the same skins, besides which they more decently wear an apron of the same kind, about a foot wide, with some threads formed into a fringe. They likewise bind their legs in the same manner with the men.

The underlip of these women is swelled out into three *fascias*, or risings, two of which issue from the corners of the mouth to the lowest part of the beard[z], and the third from the highest point, and middle of that point to the lower, like the others[a], leaving between each a space of clear flesh, which is much larger in the young than in the older women, whose faces are generally covered with punctures[b], so as to be totally disfigured.

On their necks they wear various fruits[c], instead of beads; some of these ornaments also consist of the bones of animals, or shells from the sea-coast.

This tribe of Indians is governed by a ruler, who directs where they shall go both to hunt and fish for what the community stands in need of. We also observed that one of these Indians always examined carefully the sea-shoar, when we went

[x] Copa de timbras.

[y] Colgadas par las mesillas.

[z] That is, I suppose, what would be beard in men.

[a] I must own, that I do not thoroughly comprehend this description, though I think I cannot have mis-translated it.

[b] *Picadura*, so that I conclude these swellings on the face, in such forms as described, must be occasioned by a sort of *tattooing*.

[c] Rather seeds perhaps.

to our ships on the close of twilight[d], the occasion of which probably was to take care that all their people should return safe to their habitations about that time.

It should seem that the authority of this ruler is confined to a particular village of these habitations, together with such a district of country as may be supposed to belong to the inhabitants of such a community, who sometimes are at war with other villages, against whom they appeared to ask our assistance, making us signs[e] for that purpose. There are however many other villages which are friendly to each other, if not to these Indians; for on our first arrival more than 300 came down in different parties, with their women and children, who were not indeed permitted to enter the village of our Indians.

Whilst this sort of intercourse continued between us, we observed an infant who could scarcely be a year old, shooting arrows from a bow proportioned to his size and strength, and who hit one's hand at two or three yards distance, if it was held up for a mark.

We never observed that these Indians had any idols, or made sacrifices: but as we found out that they had a plurality of wives, or women, at least, we inferred, *with good reason, that they were perfect atheists.*

Upon the death of one of these Indians they raised a sort of funeral cry, and afterwards burned the body within the house of their ruler; but from this we could not pronounce they were idolaters, because the cry of lamentation might proceed from affliction, and the body might have been burnt, that the corpse

[d] *A la oracion*, in the original, at which time the Spaniards usually make a short prayer.

[e] What these were is not stated.

should

should not be exposed to wild beasts; or perhaps this might have been done to avoid the stench of the deceased, when putrefaction might commence.

We were not able to understand one of their regulations, as they permitted our people to enter all their houses, except that of their ruler; and yet when we had broken through this eti-quette, we could not observe any thing different between the *palace*, and the other huts.

It was impossible for us to understand their language, for which reason we had no intercourse but by signs, and therefore both parties often continued in a total ignorance of each other's meaning: we observed however that they pronounced our words with great ease[f].

Their arms are chiefly arrows pointed with flint, and some of them with copper or iron[g], which we understood were procured from the N. and one of these was thus marked $C_{///}$. These ar-rows are carried in quivers of wood or bone, and hang from their wrist or neck.

[f] From hence it may be inferred, that these Indians pronounce gut-turally, as all the nations of Europe indeed do, except the English, French, and great part of Italy.

[g] Such are to be seen at Sir Ashton Lever's Museum from K. George's sound N. Lat. 50. which confirms the journal in their being brought from the North. I should conceive that the copper and iron here men-tioned must have originally been bartered at our forts in Hudson's Bay, with the travelling hordes of Indians who resort there at stated times. Some of our own people are also very enterprizing in their excursions, as one of them within these few years hath been as far as N. Lat. 72. W. Long. from Fort Churchill 24. where he saw an open sea. — In the same noble Museum is a most particular bow from the W. coast of Ame-rica N. Lat. 50. which exactly resembles one from the Labradore Coast.

But

But what they chiefly value is iron, and particularly knives or hoops of old barrels; they also readily barter for bugles, whilst they rejected both provisions or any article of dress. They pretended however that they sometimes approved the former, in order to procure our esteem; but soon after they had accepted any sort of meat, we observed that they set it aside, as of no value. At last indeed they took kindly to our biscuits, and really eat them.

Amongst these Indians there was one who had more familiar intercourse with us than all the rest, sitting down with us in sight of his countrymen.

They used tobacco, which they smoaked in small wooden pipes, in form of a trumpet, and procured from little gardens where they had planted it[h].

They chiefly hunt deer, cibulos, sea-wolves, and otters, nor did we observe that they pursued any others. The only birds we met with on this part of the coast were daws, hawks, very small paroquets, ducks, and gulls; there were also some parrots with red feet, bills, and breasts, like lories both in their heads and flight.

The fish on that coast are chiefly sardines, pejerey[i], and cod; of which they only bring home as much as will satisfy the wants of the day.

We tried to find if they had ever seen other strangers, or ships than our own, but though we took great pains to inform ourselves on this head, we never could perfectly comprehend what they said; upon the whole we conceived that we were the only foreigners who had ever visited that part of the coast.

[h] It need scarcely be observed that tobacco is an indigenous plant in N. America, as it is also of Asia.

[i] In this and other instances where I do not know the animal alluded to, I shall give the Journalist's name.

We

We likewise endeavoured to know from them whether they had any mines or precious stones; but in this we were likewise disappointed.

What we saw of the country leaves us no doubt of its fertility, and that it is capable of producing all the plants of Europe. In most of the gullies of the hills there are rills of clear and cool water, the sides of which are covered with herbs (as in the meadows of Europe) of both agreeable verdure and smell[i]. Amongst these were Castilian roses, smallage, lilies, plantain, thistles, camomile, and many others. We likewise found strawberries, rasberries, blackberries, sweet onions, and potatoes, all which grew in considerable abundance, and particularly near the rills. Amongst other plants we observed one which much resembled percely (though not in its smell), which the Indians bruised and eat, after mixing it with onions.

The hills were covered with very large, high, and strait pines, amongst which I observed some of 120 feet[k] high, and 4 in diameter towards the bottom.

All these pines are proper for masts and ship-building.

The outline of the port is represented in Chart the 6th[l], which was drawn by D. Bruno Heceta, D. Juan Fr. de la Bodega, and myself. Though the port is there represented as open, yet it is to be understood that the harbour is well sheltered from the S.W.W. & N.W. as also from the N.N.E. & E.

[This discovery was made by the schooner on the 9th of June.]

---

[i] Perhaps the accounts given by navigators of the beauty of a country or its productions after a long voyage may be not entirely relied upon, as they are commonly exagerated.

[k] Sesanta varas.

[l] These Charts, which amount to nine, have never been transmitted to England.

In

In the W. part there is a hill 50 fathoms[m] high, joining to the continent on the N. side, where there is another rising of 20, both of which afford protection not only from the winds, but the attack of an enemy.

At the entrance of the port is a small island of considerable height, without a single plant upon it; and on the sides of the coast are high rocks, which are very convenient for disembarking[n]; goods also may be shipped so near the hill[o], that a ladder may be used from the land to the vessel; and near the sand are many small rocks, which secure the ship at anchor from the S. E. and S.W.

We compleated our watering very early from the number of rills which emptied themselves into the harbour; we were likewise as soon supplied with wood.

We paid great attention to the tides, and found them to be as regular as in Europe.

We made repeated observations with regard to the latitude of this harbour, and found it was exactly 41 degrees and 7 minutes N. whilst we supposed the Longitude to be 19 degrees and 4 minutes W. of S. Blas.

We had thus thoroughly investigated every thing which relates to this harbour, except the course of a river which came from the S.W. and which appeared whilst we were at the top of the hill[p]. We took therefore the boat on the 18th, and found that the mouth was wider than is necessary for the discharge of the water, which is lost in the sands on each side, so that we

---

[m] Tuessas.
[n] By the water being deep close to these rocks.
[o] Sc. That of fifty fathoms in height.
[p] The going thither hath been before mentioned.

could

could not even enter it except at full tide.   However we left our boat, and proceded a league into the country, whilst the river continued of the same width; viz. 20 feet, and about five deep.

On the banks of this river were larger timber trees than we had before seen, and we conceived that in land-floods the whole plain (which was more than a quarter of a league broad) must be frequently covered with water, as there were many places where it continued to stagnate.

We gave this river the name of *Pigeons*, because at our first landing we saw large flocks of these, and other birds, some of which had pleasing notes.

On the sides of the mountains we found the same plants and fruits, as in the more immediate neighbourhood of Trinity-Harbour.


On the 19th of June, at 8 in the morning, we took up our anchors, and sailed with a gentle breeze from N.W. which had continued in the same direction all the time we were in port.   It fell calm however at ten, on which we cast anchor about a cannon's shot from the little island, where we had ten fathom water, and a muddy bottom.

On the 20th in the evening the wind blew again from the N.W. and we sailed to the E.S.W. *&* S.E. the wind continuing N.W. which made the sea run high.

On the 21st was new moon, and the wind veered about to the W. with small rains and mists, which separated the two ships for six or eight hours, during which we made our signals by lights, and firing guns.

In order to get into the course we were to steer, if the wind proved favourable, I mentioned to our commander what I had

read

read in D. Juan Perez's journal[q], which had been delivered to him, where it was observed that this navigator had the winds from the S. & S. E. with which it was easy to run along the coast, to a high Northern latitude, and for that reason Perez was of opinion that the coast should not be approached till 49, in which I agreed with him. Our commanders indeed kept as much to windward as possible in order to take advantage of the wind, when it should become fair; but it soon changed to the W. & N.W. which drove us on that part of the coast which we wanted to avoid.

On this same day we repaired several damages which our ship had suffered, with the greatest alacrity, in hopes of prosecuting our discoveries, and found that she sailed better comparatively with the frigate than she had done before[r].

On the 2d of July some other damages were repaired.

Although we laid great stress upon getting to the Westward, in order that we might afterwards proceed N. as also discover some port in a lower latitude than 65, yet we were not able to effect this, as the wind from being W. turned to the N.W. and drove us upon the coast [too early].

On the 9th of July I conceived myself to be in the latitude of the mouth of a river[s], discovered by John de Fuca (according to the French map) which we therefore endeavoured to make for, whilst at the same time we observed that the sea was coloured, as in soundings; many fish[t], reeds 20 feet long, and the *Orange-*

---

[q] It appears afterwards that this D. Juan Perez was *ensign* on board the frigate, and that he had sailed in a former voyage of discovery to a considerable N. Latitude on the W. coast of America.

[r] The particulars of these repairs, as also in what respect she sailed better, are omitted as uninteresting.

[s] Perhaps *gulf* [boca].

[t] *Toninas*, supposed to be porpesses.

*heads*

*heads*" likewise appeared; all of which circumstances shewed that we were not far distant from the coast.

The same day both wind and sea increased so much that our deck was thoroughly wetted, and our cistern of water also was much damaged, on which account it became necessary to steer S.W. from five in the evening till day-break, when the sea became more calm, and wind more fair; so that we sailed N. and a point to the E. hoping to discover the land.

At sun-set the horizon was more clear, and the signs of approaching the coast greatly increased; as we could not distinguish it however we kept in the wake of the frigate, by very clear moonlight.

On the 11th at day break the sky was very bright, there was an appearance of soundings, much sea-weed, many birds, and the greatest signs of being near land. In effect at 11 the sun shone, and we distinguished the coast to the N.W. when we were about 12 leagues from it.

In the evening both wind and sea rose so much that the frigate thought it right to keep us in sight, and we were much fatigued by the violence of the weather.

On the 12th we had got five or six leagues to the N. of the frigate, whilst we were but three leagues from the land, with a more favourable wind and calmer sea, so that we joined her by eleven. At six in the evening the coast was not more distant than a league, when we distinguished various headlands, many small islands, as also mountains covered with snow.

We likewise found a barren island about half a league in circumference, which we called *de Dolores*.

<hr>

" A sea-plant before described.

We

We now carried all the sail we could to follow the frigate, but we could not do so at the proper distance, in so much that at sun-set we lost sight of her, and although during the whole night we hung out lights, fired our guns, as also rockets, she never answered our signals, from which we concluded that they could not be distinguished by our companion.

On the 13th however the frigate appeared at a great distance, and seemed to be making for the coast.

We now sounded, and found 30 fathoms of water, casting anchor two leagues and half from the land.  At twelve on the same day we saw the frigate still at a greater distance to leeward, though she endeavoured to approach the coast.  On this we set sail to join her, keeping at the same time as near to the land as we could, and being not farther distant than a mile, we plainly distinguished, as we passed to the S.W. the plains, small de-tached rocks, and low headlands, till six in the evening.  As we could not however find any port, and could not bear to lose the Northing we had gained with so much trouble, we determined to cast anchor near a point, where we thought we should be able to procure wood and water, as well as masts.

The frigate was now not more than half a league distant, and we therefore made a signal to her to cast anchor, having eight fathoms of water upon sounding.

After this I soon went on board the frigate, the Captain of which told me that the Commander of the schooner should come to him, in order to hold a council, whether the schooner should proceed or not to a higher latitude, as every minute we stayed longer on the coast, would subject us to greater risques, both from the winds and sea.  This was also the more to be dreaded, as the whole crew of the frigate had been sick for the two last days, whilst the commander himself was far from well.  The

captain

captain of the schooner therefore was to keep near, and jointly take possession of this part of the coast. I accordingly carried these orders to the schooner, whose captain directed that the next day we should join the frigate.

In the mean while nine canoes of tall and stout Indians appeared, who invited the crew of the schooner with great cordiality to eat, drink, and sleep with them.

Our commander took care to regale them in the best manner he could, and particularly their chieftains, as well as those who came the most readily on board, giving them whatever they seemed most to desire.

The Indians, being obliged by these civilities, rowed near to our ship, making friendly signs, and as we answered by the same civilities, they left us at nine, and soon returned with fish of many sorts, *pagro*, whale, and salmon, as also flesh of several animals, well cured under ground. These presents, in sufficient abundance, were offered to our commander, after which they returned to their villages, leaving us in high admiration of their noble proceedings.

On the 14th in the morning the sea ebbed so low, that the ridges of rocks appeared along the coast, which prevented us from then sailing, and obliged us to wait for the full of the tide, which was to happen at 12 at noon. During this interval the Indians trafficked with us for various skins of animals, for which they expected some peices of iron in exchange, which they manifested by putting their hands upon the rudder-irons[x]; our people therefore procured them such, from old chests, after which they returned to their village, making the same signs as they had done the day before.

On

On the 1st of July we were to go on shore by order of our commander; and as we were still to continue our voyage for some time, it was necessary we should procure a sufficient quantity of water (so much being used since we sailed from Port Trinity) though hitherto we had not been able to effect this from want of a proper tide, which at the same time prevented us from getting wood and a mast. For this reason such part of the crew was pitched upon who were likely to be most active in the service, each of them taking a gun and pistol, and some of them a cutlass[y] and cartridge-box, the whole party being put under the command of Pedro Santa-Ana[z], who always distinguished himself upon such occasions. They also took with them hatchets, and were directed to send us back the boat, that we might fill it with casks, after which they were to carry them to that part of the coast where they could soonest compleat their watering.

Our detachment therefore contrived to land where there was the deepest water, and the nearest possible to a river. They had scarcely done this, however, when the Indians rushed out from the mountains to the number of 300, and surrounding our seamen immediately, we concluded that the whole detachment would have been cut off, as we only perceived a single fire from our people, and that two of them running to the shore threw themselves into the sea, whose fate we could not know on account of the shallows of the coast.

As we therefore could not help our comrades, by not having sufficient depth of sea for our vessel, we fired our great guns and

[y] Sabre.

[z] He is stated to have been contro-maestre, or perhaps master's mate.

muskets;

muskets; but as our shot did not reach the Indians, nor could they know what damage we might do them at a less distance, they did not move at all, or desist from their treacherous attack. On this, not being able to succour our comrades, we hoisted a signal of distress, which the frigate being so far off could not distinguish. The Indians however at eleven returned to their villages, whilst we neither could see our seamen or their boats.

By twelve at noon it was full sea, and we endeavoured to reach the frigate, every one exerting themselves to the utmost; our whole crew, indeed, now consisted of but five men and a boy, who were in health, with four that were sick.

As soon as we had set sail, nine canoes of Indians, with an increased number of men on board, placed themselves at a fixed distance from us, whilst one of them, with only nine chieftains[a] on board, rode pretty near to the side of our vessel, offering us, whilst their bows were unbent, some handsome jackets, and practising their former arts of deceit, by tempting us with the provisions they had before supplied.

But we were now upon our guard, and preparing for our defence, though we still thought it right on our part to entice them nearer, by shewing bugles and other trifles, which had as little effect upon our enemies, who contrived however to make signs that we should go on shore. At last they were tired of these overtures, and knowing the small number of our crew, they made a shew of surrounding our vessel; holding their bows bent against us.

On the other hand, though we had but three on board able to handle a musquet (viz. our Captain, his servant, and myself)

---

[a] So the original; and I conclude the meaning to be, that in this canoe there were none but chieftains.

yet

yet we soon killed six of the Indiàns, as also damaged their canoe. They now experienced how much we were able to annoy them, and seemed to be astonished. They afterwards covered their dead with their jackets, and at last returned to such a distance that we could not reach them with our shot; in which retreat they were assisted by the other canoes, who had not before supported them. They then held a council, which ended in their going back to their village.

Our commander, in the mean time, hearing the discharge of our musquets, thought we should want ammunition, and sent us some in the launch, in which we cast anchor along side of the frigate. We then went on board, hoping that we should be permitted to use the launch, land with an armèd force, destroy the villages of the Indians, and try to recover those of our own people, who perhaps had hid themselves in the woods, or had saved themselves by swimming.

On this point we held a council, at which the commander stated our dangerous situation, the difficulties in landing we were to expect, both from sea and weather, and the distance of the village; he also added, that the destruction of our people was almost distinctly seen, and therefore that there could be little probability of any one's having escaped.

D. Cristoval de Revilla and D. Juan Perez were of opinion we should directly sail, although the commander[b] and myself pressed taking some revenge for the butchery of our comrades, as likewise waiting to know the fate of those who might have survived by swimming, and who must necessarily surrender themselves to the Barbarians. We also dwelt upon the strong presumption, that it would be agreeable to his majesty that the In-

[b] The commander seems to have given different advice before.

dians

dians should feel the superior force of his arms, who would otherwise treat future discoverers in the same manner; we added, that though the village was not near, yet if we waited till next day we might reach it, whilst it might be expected that the winds would not blow with violence at the new moon.

The reasons on both sides having been thus urged, the commander readily consented to follow the advice and wishes of the majority.

When this point was decided, our commander took our opinions with regard to the schooner's proceeding, as she was in so bad plight; when (except D. Cristoval de Revilla) we all agreed that she should continue to prosecute her voyage. These our opinions were reduced into writing on the 16th.

[These are again omitted, as probably uninteresting to the reader: but both the captain of the schooner, and the journalist agreeing to proceed;]

On the 14th of July we sailed, at five in the evening, from this road, which lies in 47. 21 N. Lat[c]. the wind being N.W. and N.N.W. by which we left the coast, steering S.W.

On the 19th our captain received some letters from Don Juan Perez (ensign[d] of the frigate) as likewise the surgeon, in which they stated the then health of their crew, and desiring our opinion thereon.

[Here follow the answers of the captain of the schooner and Maurelle the journalist, who, to their great credit, persist in their voyage of discovery.]

---

[c] The longitude is not stated, but by the ship's reckoning I find that the W. Longitude from St. Blas was 21 19.
　　[d] Alferez.

Till the 24th the wind continued N.W. & N. when the schooner received from the frigate a cannon, with a box of powder and ball.

From the 24th to the 30th we steered N.W. when at sunset there were great threatenings of a storm, and the weather becoming dark, the sea ran so high, that we could not distinguish the lights of the frigate, and were obliged to make our signals by guns and rockets.

On the 31st it continued to be so dark that even during the day we could not see the frigate.

On the 1st of August at day-break we had the same dark weather, so that we could not distinguish at half a league's distance, nor had we sight of the frigate: we kept on however (the wind abating) with a Westerly course, till the 4th, when we supposed ourselves to be 17 leagues W. of the continent.

On the 5th the wind began to be favourable from the S.W. and the frigate still not appearing, our captain consulted us whether we should prosecute our discoveries. We had indeed for the last two months been reduced to short allowance of provisions, and a quart of water each day, since we left the last land; our bread also was almost spoiled by the sea getting into the bread-room, and the season for sailing to the Northward began almost to end. Yet notwithstanding these, and other objections, we continued unanimously of opinion to execute our orders; as, if we did otherwise, his majesty must have incurred the expence of a fresh expedition, Our crew likewise was now animated, and every one agreed to contribute proportionably for a solemn mass to our Lady of Bethlem, intreating her that we might be able to reach the Latitude enjoined by our instructions. This proposal of the crew being communicated to the captain, he applauded much their ardour and devotion, which was rewarded before evening, by the winds blowing from a favourable quarter.

On

On the 10th there was a full moon, and the wind blew fresh from the S.W.

On the 13th we conceived ourselves to be in soundings from the colour of the sea; at the same time appeared *Orange heads*, many flags, many birds, with red feet, breast, and beak, as also many whales; all which were certain signs of our nearer approach to land.

During the 14th and 15th these signs increased, when we found ourselves in N. Lat. 56, 8. & 154 leagues W. of the continent, and 69 leagues from an island to be found in our chart[e], which likewise pointed out an archipelago in the same parallel. This search however was attended with great difficulty, as the wind blew with great violence, whilst the mists did not permit us to distinguish any distant object.

At noon on the 16th we saw land to the N.W. at the distance of six leagues, and it soon afterwards opened to the N.E. presenting considerable headlands and mountains, one of which was of an immense height, being situated upon a projecting cape, and of the most regular and beautiful form I had ever seen. It was also quite detached from the great ridge of mountains. Its top was covered with snow, under which appeared some wide gullies, which continue till about the middle of the mountain, and from thence to the bottom are trees of the same kind as those at Trinity.

We named this moutain *St. Jacinthus*[g] and the cape *del Enganno*[h], both of which are situated in N. Lat. 57. 2. and by two

---

[e] I should rather suppose that this was the chart of D. Juan Perez, who was on board, and had been on a former voyage of discovery.

[f] Before described to be pines.

[g] There is a monastery of *St. Jacinthus*, at a small distance from Mexico. Gage's Survey of the W. Indies.

[h] Or of deceit.

repeated

repeated observations at a mile's distance we found the W. Long. from St. Blas to be 34. 12.

From this cape we fixed the principal points on the coast, as will appear by our chart.

On the 17th the wind blew moderate from the S. by means of which we entered a bay that was three leagues wide at its mouth, and which was protected from the N. by cape *del Enganno*; on the opposite side to this cape we discovered a port more than a league wide at the entrance, perfectly secure from all winds but the S. We nearly approached the sides of this bay, and never found less than fifty fathoms in depth; but we could not perceive any kind of flat or plain, as the mountains come quite down to the shore. Notwithstanding this we distinguished a small river, which (it being night) we did not further attend to, but cast anchor in 66 fathoms, the bottom being a clay, as we found upon drawing up our anchors.

This port is situated in 57. 11 N. Lat. and 34. 12. W. Long. from S. Blas; which, together with the headland, we named Guadelupe.

On the 18th we sailed again, with little wind; when two canoes, with four Indians in each, appeared (viz. two men and two women) who, however, did not seem to wish to come on board us, but only made signs that we should go on shore.

We continued our course however (the wind being N.W.) till nine in the morning, when we entered another port, not so large indeed, but the adjacent country much more desirable to navigators, as a river empties itself here of eight or ten feet wide, whilst the harbour is protected from almost every wind, by means of a long ridge of high islands, almost joining each other, with anchorage of 18 fathoms, the bottom being a sand. Here we cast anchor at a pistol's shot from the land, where we saw, on

the

the bank of the river, a high house, and a parapet[i] of timber supported by stakes drove into the ground, where we observed ten Indian men, besides women and children.

We named this port *de los Remedios*, and found that it was situated in 57. 18 N. Lat. and 34. 12 W. Long. from St. Blas.

The same day, having prepared ourselves for defence against the Indians, five of us landed about noon, when, having posted ourselves in the safest place we could fix upon, we planted the cross with all proper devotion, cutting another on a rock[k], and displaying the Spanish colours, according *to our instructions* on that head.

When we had thus taken possession of the country we advanced quite to the bank of the river, in order to fix upon the most convenient place for water, which we were in great want of, as well as still greater of wood; so that we were under an absolute necessity of providing ourselves with both. Having fixed upon the proper spot, we now returned to the ship, the Indians having not come forth from their parapet.

We soon however perceived them approach the place where we had fixed the cross, which they took away, and fixed it on the front of their house, in the proper direction, whilst at the same time they made us signs with their open arms, that they had thus taken possession of our cross.

On the 19th we landed at a point somewhat distant, to procure wood and a mast, whilst we secured our retreat by a proper disposition of swivels and musquetry.

Afterwards we returned to the mouth of the river, to fill our barrels with water, when the Indians hung out a white leaf[i] from

---

[i] Probably this was a stage for curing fish, of which these Indians soon offered a present to the Spaniards.

a pole, fixed very near to their house, and advancing to the opposite bank without any arms, they made several signs, which we did not comprehend. We however signified to them in the best manner we could that we came only for water[m]; on which the chieftain of the Indians, conceiving that we were very dry, brought with him a cup of it, with some cured fish, as far as the middle of the river, where it was received by one of our seamen, who directed the Indian to present the water and fish to our captain, who immediately returned him in exchange bugles and small pieces of cloth. The Indians however were not to be so satisfied, but insisted on other barter for the water, which we refusing on our part, they threatened us with long and large lances pointed with flint, which we paid no other attention to but that of securing our post. Our assailants at last finding that

we

[m] The behaviour of these Indians in their intercourse with the Spaniards seems to prove a rather superior degree of civilization, than is generally experienced from Barbarians.

We find by this account, that the Spaniards, having fixed a cross upon their ground, the Indians resent this mark of ownership, and (as a Spaniard would have done in his own country if his neighbour thus endeavoured to make good a claim) immediately remove the cross; in which the laws of Europe would certainly have supported them. The leaving any symbol of possession upon an uninhabited and uncultivated district may indeed give a right against posterior claimants who cannot set up a better; but this part of the American continent was not only peopled, but we are informed a house and fishing-stage had been built upon it.

We find by this journal, that the Viceroy of Mexico most particularly enjoined by his instructions that possession should be thus taken, conceiving probably that the converting Indians to the Christian faith, entitles the converter to every thing which may belong to the converts. This flimsy right however could not be maintained an instant even upon this ground, in any Court of common sense, for the Spaniards neither intended then, or hereafter, to make a settlement in this Northern Latitude, without which it is impossible that such pious intentions could be accomplished.

The

we did not wish to surround them, but held them in contempt, went back to their houses, as we did to our ship, having procured the wood and single mast which we wanted, though not so much water as would have been convenient; but we did not think it right to carry away more, that we might not further irritate the inhabitants.

At the mouth of the river there was abundance of fish, of which our people caught many whilst we were on shore, and we could have procured a sufficient quantity to have lasted us a great while, had we been prepared with proper tackle. They were well tasted, and in vast numbers.

The mountains were covered with the same sort of pines as at *Trinity:* the inhabitants also use the same dress, only rather longer; they likewise wear a cap over their hair, which covers their whole head.

The Spaniards, after this, inform the Indians, by signs, that they want water, on which one of the Americans brings a cup thus filled, with some cured fish, half way across the river, and stops there till a Spaniard advances the other half to receive it, whilst bugles and other trifles are offered in exchange by the Spaniards, and refused by the Indians, who insist on a better sort of payment.

It is evident, by the presents of the cup of water* and cured fish, that the Indians wished to supply all the wants of these strangers as far as they were able, notwithstanding they had thus endeavoured to gain a wrongful possession of their country; they seem therefore to have had a right to that species of barter which they stood most in need of.

This contempt for bugles, and other trifles, offered by the Spaniards, is a further proof of the civilization of these Indians, whose progenitors, it should seem, must be rather looked for on the Asiatic, than Labradore coast, as I am informed that they have beards, which the Indians of the central and Eastern coast of N. America have not. It is said indeed by some, that these Indians eradicate their beard from its earliest appearance; but I can as little believe that this can be effected by any industry, as that they could by any art or pains make hair grow upon the palms of their hands.

* I am informed, that the inhabitants of K. George's Sound, on this same coast, insisted upon Capt. Cook's paying for the grass he had cut.

We

We found the weather excessively cold, with much rain and fogs, nor did we see the sun for the three days we continued here. At the same time we had only faint land-breezes; from all which circumstances, as well as the great fatigue of our seamen, little cover from the bad weather, and great want of proper cloaks to keep them warm, our ship's company so sickened, that we could only muster two men for every watch.

On the 21st we steered N.W. the wind being at S. E. in order to discover whether there was any land to the E. when we might reach two degrees of higher latitude to the N. or whether it did not lie to the W. which we conceived to be more probable.

On the 22d we knew, by our reckoning, that we must be near the Eastern part of the coast[m], as we found ourselves by an observation at noon to be in 57. 18 N. Lat.

At two in the evening the wind blew fresh at N.W. when we wanted to gain so much Westing as to permit the reaching a higher Northern Latitude, in which attempt we must have therefore lost many days, whilst the season for prosecuting our discoveries drew so near to an end. To this it must be added, that the sickness of our crew increased every day, by their great fatigues, on which account we desisted from our Northern course, and steered S. E. approaching the coast at a less distance than a mile, and endeavouring to observe every projection of it.

Though we now therefore determined to return to S. Blas, yet we comforted ourselves in having reached so high a latitude as 58[n], beyond what any other Navigators had been able to effect in those seas, though our vessel sailed so indifferently that we often had thoughts of quitting her.

[m] Sc. as laid down by Bellin.

[n] By the table only 57. 57. Capt. Cook however is said to have traced the W. coast of America beyond 60 N. Lat. when it runs for some degrees nearly E.

In

In sailing along the coast we took indefatigable pains to observe with precision how it lay, from which innumerable objections offered themselves to M. Bellin's Charts.

This engineer hath chiefly founded himself upon the tracks of two Russian Navigators, Beering and Tschirikow, who were sent upon discoveries in 1741. It is evident however that the Russian maps are not to be depended upon, for if they had been tolerably accurate we should have fallen in with the land to the Westward, more easily than to the East[o].

Bellin is not less erroneous in laying down the American coast, and indeed it is not at all extraordinary that his errors should be so numerous, as he had no materials for his charts, but his own fruitful imagination; no navigator having visited many parts of the American continent in these high latitudes but ourselves.

We now attempted to find out the straits[p] of Admiral Fonte, though as yet we had not discovered the Archipelago of S. Lazarus, through which he is said to have sailed.

With this intent we searched every bay and recess of the coast, and sailed round every headland, lying to during the night, that we might not lose sight of this entrance; after these pains taken, and being favoured by a N.W. wind[q], it may be pronounced that no such straits are to be found.

On the 24th at 2 in the evening, and being in 55. 17 N. Lat. *we doubled a cape, and entered into a large bay, discovering to*

[o] The journalist seems to speak here with regard to the then situation of the schooner  Other objections follow to Bellin s map, which cannot be comprehended without having the chart before one.

[p] Entrada, or entrance into them rather. In a map which I have procured, this entrance is laid down in N. Lat. 48. and said to have been discovered by Juan de Fuca in 1592.

[q] It must now be recollected that the schooner is returning to S. Blas.

the

the N. an arm of the sea, where the temperature was very unpleasant[r], but the sea perfectly calm, being sheltered from the wind. This *arm* also affords excellent water from rills and pools, whilst the anchorage is good, with a vast plenty of fish. It is delineated in one of our charts.

As we were now becalmed, the schooner rowed till we cast anchor in the entrance or mouth, the water being 20 fathoms, and the bottom soft mud. At this time we were not more than two musquet shots from the land, and wished to lay down the interior parts, but were not able to effect this for want of wind. We now experienced a pleasant temperature, which probably arose from some large volcanoes, the light of which we perceived during the night, though at a considerable distance. This unexpected warmth totally restored the health of our crew[s].

As we thus lay at anchor, and so much to our satisfaction, our Captain gave me orders (being himself indisposed) that I.should land with some of our crew, and with the same precautions as at *Los Remedios*. He also directed me to take possession for his Majesty of this part of the coast, and name it Bucarelly[t]. I accordingly obeyed his instructions in all particulars, without seeing a single Indian, though there were the following proofs of the country's being inhabited; viz. a hut, some paths, and a wooden outhouse[u]. On the 24th we went a second time on shore, and provided ourselves with as much wood and water as we wanted.

[r] It is to be supposed on account of the cold.
[s] It must be recollected, that they were now sheltered from the wind as well as warmed by the Vulcanoes.
[t] Then Viceroy of Mexico.
[u] Corral.

We

We made two observations on different days, and found our latitude to be 55. 17. and W. Long. from S. Blas 32. 9.

The mountains near this port or inlet are covered with the same trees as those at the other places, where we had landed, but I can say nothing with regard to the inhabitants, from what hath been before stated.

To the S. we saw an island of a moderate height, at the distance of six leagues, which we named S. Carlos, and sailed on the 29th with a gentle breeze at N. but which fell calm at noon, when we were opposite to a bare island, which scarcely appeared above the sea; there are many rocks however, both to the E. and W. Here we anchored in 22 fathoms, and about two leagues distant from the island of S. Carlos.

In this situation we observed a Cape, which we named St. Augustine, at the distance of four or five leagues; after which the coast trended to the E. so much that we lost sight of it. We found also that there were here such violent currents in opposite directions, that we could not sound. As these currents rose and fell with the tide, it should seem that this inlet hath no communication but with the sea.

This cape S. Augustine is nearly in 55 N. Lat. and we having heard that in a former voyage D. Juan Perez had discovered an arm of the sea in this same parallel, where there were many currents, we justly concluded this must be the same, though several seamen who were in that voyage, did not recollect either the cape or mountains in the neighbourhood, but this probably arose from their not approaching them in the same direction.

What we observed on this part of the coast strongly inclined us to have a more perfect knowledge of it; the wind however (it being new moon) became variable, and fixed at last in the S.W.

We

We concluded that it would thus continue till the full[x], which would prevent us from approaching the mouth of this bay, and consequently make it impossible to explore the sides of it. We likewise considered that we were now in such a latitude that we might easily reach 60 degrees if the wind was favourable[y], that moreover we were provided with what we had occasion for, that the health of our crews was re-established, and that for all these reasons it would be better to attempt reaching the highest Latitude we could.

To these arguments it was added, that we should have fewer difficulties in this trial from our knowledge of the coast; and this measure being thus resolved upon, the two ships divided some cloaths[z] (which the schooner had on board, to truck with the Indians at Port Trinity) so that our people seemed now to have forgotten all their sufferings. We accordingly sailed, steering N.W.

On the 28th the wind was variable, obliging us to approach the coast at 55. 50. when it fixed in the evening to the S.W. according to our wishes.

On the 29th and 30th the wind was S. though often veering to the S.W. with occasional squalls and tornadoes, accompanied by high seas, which drove us on the coast in 56. 70. from whence we clawed off with the land breeze and tornadoes, in which disagreeable situation we continued till the first of September.

During the two preceding days six of our crew were seized with strong symptoms of the scurvy, which not only shewed

---

[x] The Spaniards, during this voyage, seem to have paid great attention to the moon, as having an effect upon the wind.

[y] A S.W. was so.

[z] This additional cloathing was probably thought necessary, as the ships were now to sail N. whilst the winter was approaching.

itself

itself in their gums, but from the great swellings on their legs they had lost the use of them. From this calamity we could only muster two on each guard, one of which steered, and the other handled the sails. We unfortunately caught this terrib¹ distemper from the seamen of the frigate, with whom we had occasional communication. In consequence of this distress we agreed now to return, making as many observations as we could in relation to the lying of the coast.

At the beginning of September the wind was variable, but on the 6th it fixed in the S.W. blowing with such force that at midnight we were obliged to take in all our sails, and turn the ship's head to the S. whilst the wind and sea increased, in so much that at two in the morning of the 7th neither vessel could resist its violence, though we each endeavoured to keep where we were, on account of the coast being at so small a distance.

Whilst we were thus employed a sea broke in, which damaged most of our stores. [The particulars of other damage to parts of the ship here follows, but is omitted for reasons that have been before mentioned.]

On this same day (viz. 7th of September), both wind and sea became more calm; on which we steered E. from 6 in the evening till day-break of the next day, when the wind was favourable from the N.W. and we pursued our intentions of falling in again with the coast, in Lat. 55. finding ourselves, since the storm, with only one seaman who could stand to the helm, whilst the captain or myself managed the sails.

The wind continuing favourable, our captain endeavoured to cheer those who were sick, but we could only prevail upon two of them who were recovering to assist us during the day; as for the master's mate, we conceived that he would die.

On

On the 11th we saw land, at the distance of eight or nine leagues, and in Lat. 53. 54. but as we wished not to approach so near as not to be able to leave it, on account of our having so few hands capable of working, we kept at a proper distance, only having a view of it from day to day, and not examining its capes, bays, and ports.

In Lat. 49. however we endeavoured to draw nearer to the land, both because we were persuaded that the wind would continue favourable, and that some of the convalescents might now begin to assist us; so that in Lat. 47. 43. we were not farther distant than a mile, when we attended to all proper particulars[a], as before.

On the 20th, at eight in the morning, we were within half a league, precisely in the same situation as on the 13th of July; we found however 17 leagues difference with regard to our Longitude.

On the 21st, being still nearer the coast, the wind blew from the S. *&* S.W. which, though moderate, obliged us to sail from the land.

On the 22d the wind was N.W. but as both the captain and myself were ill of a fever, the ship steered for the port of Monterey. This our sickness made the rest of the crew almost despair; for which reason the captain and myself shewed ourselves upon the deck as often as we could, in which efforts the Almighty assisted us.

On the 24th, finding ourselves somewhat better, we discovered the land in 45. 27. sailing along the coast at about the distance of a cannon's shot; and as we therefore could distinctly see every considerable object, we lay to during the night,

---

[a] That is, for laying the coast down in their charts.

hoping

hoping thus to find the river of Martin Aquilar, and continued this search till we were in Lat. 45. 50. when we distinguished a cape exactly resembling a round table, with some red gullies[b], from which the coast trends to the S.W. From this part rise ten small islands, and some others which are scarcely above the sea; the Latitude of this Cape hath before been mentioned, and its Longitude is 20. 4. W. from S. Blas. As we therefore could see nothing of Martin de Aquilar's River in this second trial, we conclude that it is not to be found, for we must have discovered it, if any such river was on this part of the coast.

It is said indeed that Aquilar observed the mouth of this river in 43[c], but the instruments of those times[d] were very imperfect. Allowing the error however to have been in making the latitude too high, and that therefore we might have found it in 42 or lower; yet this we can scarcely conceive to be the truth, as we examined all that part of the coast, except about fifty minutes of Latitude.

After this last return to the coast, we endeavoured to make for the port of S. Francisco, which having discovered in 38. 18. we entered a bay which is sufficiently sheltered from the N. and S.W. We soon afterwards distinguished the mouth of a considerable river, and some way up a large port exactly resembling a dock[e]; we therefore concluded this to be the harbour of S. Francisco (which we were in search of), as the History of California places it in 38. 4.

[b] Barancas.
[c] This is stated before, when the river was looked out for in that latitude.
[d] Viz. in 1603.
[e] Digue.

We

We wished, on this account, to enter this port, which we should have easily accomplished, if the sea had not run very high.  We began however to doubt whether this was really the harbour of S. Francisco, because we did not see any inhabitants, nor the small islands which are said to be opposite.  In this state of suspense we cast anchor near one of the points which we called *de Arenas*, in six fathoms and a clay bottom.

A vast number of Indians now presented themselves on both points[f], who passed from one to the other in small canoes made of *Fule*[g], where they talked loudly for two hours or more, till at last two of them came along side of the ship, and most liberally presented us with plumes of feathers, rosaries of bone, garments of feathers, as also garlands of the same materials, which they wore round their head, and a canister of seeds, which tasted much like walnuts.  Our captain gave them in return bugles, looking glasses[h], and peices of cloth.

These Indians are large and strong, their colour being the same as that of the whole territory[i]; their disposition is most liberal, as they seemed to expect no recompense for what they had furnished us with:  a circumstance which we had not experienced in those to the Northward.

We were not able to sound the interior parts of this port, on account of our sick, who were to be as soon as possible landed in a place of safety, in order that they might have the better chance of recovering.

[f] Sc. Those just now named by the journalist *de Arenas*.

[g] Some sort of wood, and probably well known in the province of Mexico.

[h] In the former intercourse with the more Northern Indians the Spaniards never produced this article of barter, which seems to have been ill-judged œconomy.  They were now returning however, and must have thrown away these trifles at S. Blas.

[i] It is not very clear whether the Journalist means by this of Mexico, or the whole N. Western continent of America.

Whilst

Whilst we were in this port (which we did not conceive to be that of S. Francisco) we had no further intercourse with the inhabitants, and we prepared to clear the point *de las Avenas*, in order that, with a N.W. wind, the next day we might, with less difficulty, leave this part of the coast. Having effected this, we cast anchor in six fathoms, the bottom being a clay.

This port, which we named de *la Bodega*[i], is situated in 38. 18 N. Lat. and 18. 4 W. Long. from S. Blas.

On the 4th of October, at two in the morning, on the first flow of the tide, in a contrary direction to that of the currents, the sea ran so high that our whole ship was entirely covered by it, at the same time that the boat on the side of her was broken into shivers.

There is not sufficient depth of anchorage at the mouth of this port, for a vessel to resist this violence of surge, when it is occasioned by the causes before-mentioned.

If we had been apprized of this circumstance, we should have either continued where we were first at anchor, or otherwise sailed further from the mouth of the harbour.

In all parts of this port, which we had an opportunity of sounding, the bottom is nearly of the same depth[k]. The entrance is very easy with the prevailing wind of N.W. but in leaving it, if the wind blows from the same quarter, it is necessary to get further out to sea from the *Points*[l]. If the wind blows from the S.W. E. or S. it is not necessary to take this precaution[m].

---

[i] The Captain of the Schooner. The Latitude of this harbour coincides nearly with that discovered by Sir *Francis* Drake; but the Spaniards would scarcely insert this brave heretic in their Calendar.

[k] A draft was made of this harbour.

[l] Sc. de las Arenas.

[m] Because then the wind and currents do not oppose each other.

We

We observed, that the tides in this Latitude are regular, as in Europe, it being high water at noon, when the moon is new.

The mountains near this port are entirely naked in every part of them[n]; but we observed that those more inland were covered with trees.

The plains near the sea-coast had a good verdure, and seemed to invite cultivation.

About eight in the morning of the 4th of October the sea became more calm, on which the Indians came round us as before, in their canoes, offering us the same presents, which had the same return.

At nine we set sail, and having doubled the point *del Cordon*[o] we steered S.S.W. the wind being moderate, and at W. in order to reach a Cape, which appeared to the S. at the distance of about five leagues.

On the fifth we sailed near those small islands which the charts and history of California place at the entrance of the harbour of S. Francisco; but as we were very clear that the harbour which we had just left, was not that thus called, we continued to steer N.E. (and between some of these islands) in order to reach the Cape before mentioned, when we intended to approach the coast, and look out for the port of S. Francisco.

At noon on this same day we had an observation, and found these islands to be in 37. 55. N. Lat. lying to the S.W. of the Cape at the distance of three leagues.

As soon as we reached the Cape we ran along the coast which lay to the E. and N.E. about the distance of a cannon's shot; and by six in the evening we were not above two miles distant

[n] This probably arises from their being exposed to the N.W. which is the prevailing wind.

[o] This point undoubtedly is marked in the Spanish Chart.

from

from the mouth of the harbour of St. Francis; but having no boat[p], or other convenience for this purpose, we resolved to stand for Monterey, and double another Cape, which projected still further from the coast[q].

At ten at night it fell calm; which continued till the 6th at noon, when the wind was moderate at W. and we steered S. S. W.

By eight at night the wind freshened from the N.W. with squalls and mists.

On the 7th, at eight in the morning, we conceived ourselves to be in the latitude of Monterey, which we endeavoured therefore to keep in, though the weather was so misty, that we could not see half a league.

At three in the evening we discovered the coast to the S.W. at the distance of a mile; and finding that we now entered a bay, we soon afterwards discovered the S. Carlos at anchor, and therefore knew that we were now in the port of Monterey. On this we fired some cannon, and boats immediately came out to us, by whose assistance we anchored in three fathoms, the bottom being a sand.

This port is situated in 36 44. N. Lat. & 17 W. of S. Blas.

On the 8th we landed our sick, and amongst the rest our captain and myself, who had suffered more from the scurvy than any of them. Not one of the whole crew indeed was free from this complaint.

We immediately experienced the kind offices of the Fathers established at this mission, who procured for us all the refreshments they were able, with the most perfect charity. In truth,

----

[p] It having been demolished by a heavy sea not long before.
[q] That is, than the before-mentioned Cape.

we

we could not possibly have so soon recovered from our distressed situation, but by their unparalleled attentions to our infirmities, which they removed by reducing themselves to a most pitiful allowance.

Don Fernando de Rivuera, who commanded at this port, was equally kind, in supplying our wants, so that in about a month we were pronounced to be so much better in point of health, that we determined to return to S. Blas.

We sailed therefore from Monterey on the 1st of November, and D. Bruno Heceta supplied us with some hands from the Frigate, the crew of which had not suffered so much from the scurvy as that of the schooner. At the distance however of two leagues it fell calm so that we continued in sight of the port till the 4th, the wind being at S. & S.W.

On the 4th at noon the wind was favourable from the N.W. aud we continued steering S. till the 13th when we approached the coast of California in 24. 15. N. Lat. and kept along it till Cape St. Lucas, which we left at six in the evening on the 16th.

We suppose this Cape to be in N. Lat. 22. 49. & W. Long. from S. Blas 5. 0.

On the 16th we saw the Islands of Maria, and on the 20th in the evening we cast anchor in the port of S. Blas.

Thus ended our voyage of discovery; and I trust that the fatigues and distresses which we suffered will redound to the advantage and honour of our *invincible* Sovereign, whom may God always keep under his holy protection!

FRANCISCO ANTONIO MAURELLE.

Obser-

Observations of the Journalist D. Antonio Maurelle; arising from what happened during the course of the voyage, with regard to the best method of making Discoveries on the W. coast of America, to the Northward of California.

IT may be objected, at the outset of these Observations, that the experience arising from a single voyage in those seas is not sufficient to form any solid advice on this head, which may be thoroughly depended upon. To this I answer, that our continuance on this coast was for more than eight months, and therefore must have afforded us sufficient grounds on which to build reasonable presumptions, though I cannot presume to offer them to future navigators in any stronger light.

There is no occasion to give any directions about the passage from S. Blas to Monterey, since this course hath been so frequently sailed after the establishment at the latter, and the best method of making this navigation is therefore so well known.

Suffice it then to say, that the short passage to windward, as far as the islands of Maria, is necessary, on account of the currents, which would otherwise soon carry a ship in sight of Cape St. Lucas, where probably the voyage would be retarded by calms.

Some are of opinion, that you should not sail Northward till you are considerably to the Windward of these islands; but I do not see the use of this loss of time, and think that it is sufficient just to get to the W. of them, and then steer Northerly on the very day you reach the parallel of the Marias.

In order to effect such voyage of discovery, it is necessary to gain as much W. Longitude as the winds will permit, which

blow

blow from the N.W. to the N. as far as 15 degrees W[a]. and which only permit a course to the W.N.W. E. or E.S.E. whilst often such trade wind extends still further to the W. Notwithstanding this circumstance the ship should never lie to, much less steer Eastward, as thus the voyage would be much re-tarded.

From these 15 degrees of Westing, to 30 in the same direc-tion, the wind is generally from N.E. to N. which will permit a N.W. course. It may perhaps be advisable even to get a Westing as far as 35 degrees, if the object of the voyage is to reach 55. 60. or even 65[b] of Northern Latitude, because the greater the Westing, the greater is the certainty of S. & S.W. winds, which will be so favourable to such a destination.

If when this Westing hath been gained, the winds should prove variable, I should still advise a N.E. course[c]. Under the sup-position that the discoverer wants to fall in with the coast of America, in 55 N. Lat. he should keep between 35 & 37 W. Long. till he reaches that Latitude. If, on the contrary, he wants to explore the same coast in N. Lat. 60. I should then advise a N.W. course to be pursued till he hath gained a West-ing of 39 degrees. If the navigator wishes to make discoveries even so high as 65 N. Lat. I conceive that he should then have a westing of 45 degrees, when he hath gained this parallel.

With these precautions I imagine that the persevering navigator would accomplish the height of his wishes.

---

[a] i. e. probably from S. Blas.

[b] It appears by the Journal, that they were instructed to proceed thus far N. if possible, which idea was probably taken from Ellis's Pre-face to the N. W. Passage, many extracts from which are made by Venegas, in his History of California, and particularly what relates to this supposed Latitude of 65.

[c] *en el primer quadrante*, as I conceive the Spaniards make the N. E. the first quarter ; the S. E. the second ; the S. W. the third ; and the N. W. the fourth.

As

As accidents however will happen in all voyages, which may drive the ship upon the coast in a lower latitude, I would then by all means advise to gain a Westing, as far as 200 leagues from the land. But it must be remembered that at perhaps 150 leagues W. the wind may be variable, though I am confident it cannot be depended upon, as favourable for any time, and would soon veer to the N.W. For these reasons I hold it to be absolutely necessary, that a westing of at least 200 leagues should be procured, till N. Lat. 50 is reached.

If the ship is blown upon the coast in lower latitudes, the crew not only suffers commonly from fatigue and sickness, but so much time is lost, that winter comes on before the great object of such a voyage can be compleated. I would therefore advise sailing from S. Blas at the end of January, or at latest the beginning of February; and for this additional reason, that the crew would not suffer so much from change of temperature in the different climates, if without stopping in any lower latitude, they at once come upon the coast of America in 55. Here they might rest a little from their fatigues, procure water, recover by that fine air[d] if indisposed; besides, that in this latitude there would be no occasion to lose time in procuring a further Westing, as here the winds are very variable.

It need be scarcely said, that the knowing the weather, which commonly prevails in these seas, is of much importance to navigators; and it is still less necessary to advise, that particular attention should be paid to the appearances in the horizon which

---

[d] The port of *los Remedios* is here alluded to, which is in 57. 18. and where the crew recovered very fast from the warmth of the air, attributed to Vulcanoes in the neighbourhood. S. Blas, being in N. Lat. 22. is consequently more cool in January than perhaps any month of the year, whilst they would be in 55 perhaps at Midsummer.

threaten

threaten a storm. These however are not much to be apprehended till N. Lat. 40. as between S. Blas and that parallel, such lowering clouds either disperse themselves very soon, or fall in rain, which lulls the sea.

From 40 to 50 degrees N. (supposing the ship to have gained a Westing of 200 leagues from the American coast,) these appearances are more to be watched, as in these latitudes the S. wind blows fresh, though pretty constant.

It is to be observed also, that the S.W. in these parallels is sometimes stronger than the S. for which reason I would advise not to carry much sail.

This last precaution is still more necessary in higher latitudes than 50, since the S.W. often blows so violently that it is prudent to lie to, as these squalls do not last for any time.

I also particularly advise the navigator to guard against the effects of winds from the E. which sometimes are violent in these latitudes; not but that sometimes W. winds are equally blustering, yet they are not so common, nor last so long. It should also be noticed, that the higher the latitude, the more such weather is to be apprehended.

When the coast of America *is very near*, there is no regular wind but the N.W. and this holds to the Southward from 54 N. Lat. it sometimes blows indeed fresh from this quarter, but there is no objection to this, when the ship is on its return[c].

The sea from S. Blas to 40 degrees N. Lat. runs commonly high, when the wind is at N.W. or N. but as it does not often blow with violence from this quarter, these seas are generally

---

[c] It must be remembered, that for this reason the Journalist advises the navigator who wants to reach a high N. Latitude, to gain so large a Westing from the coast of America.

navigable.

navigable. From Lat. 40 to 50 (when near the coast) the sea often runs still higher, meeting the tide from the shoar, but I do not mean to raise too great apprehensions on this account.

At the distance however of 100 leagues from the coast the seas are often still heavier; so that I would advise lying to, if the wind is not favourable.

From 50 degrees upwards the seas rise proportionably with the winds, particularly if they blow from the S. or S.W. but soon become calm when the weather clears.

[Here follow some observations, with regard to the effect of the moon upon the weather, which I shall not translate, as the influence of this planet in such respect seems now to be much exploded.]

As approaches to the coast ought always to put the navigator on his guard, he may depend upon the following signs for its not being far distant.

When the coast is about 80 or 90 leagues to the E. those sea-plants appear which I have before called *Orange heads*; but I must now add, that from the state of them, as they float, one may sometimes infer, that the land is not so far distant.

Its figure much resembles the fistular stalk of garlick[e]; and from the top of its head hang some long leaves, by which the plant is fixed to the rocks. Now if these leaves are tolerably perfect, they afford a strong presumption, that they have not floated far from the coast. On the contrary, those which have been wafted to a considerable distance, have generally lost this head, and the stalk becomes more rough, when you may suppose that you are 50 leagues from the land.

[e] The appearance of this plant on the coast of California, is noticed in Lord Anson's Voyage.

At

At the same distance the sea begins to indicate, by its colour, that you are in soundings, but this circumstance requires some attention and habit; when you are not more than 30 or 40 leagues from the coast, this appearance is much more distinguishable, though if you was to cast anchor you would not find any bottom.   In this same situation you will likewise perceive birds, sea-wolves[f], otters, and whales, together with the plant Zacate del Mar before-mentioned, which hath long and narrow leaves.   When these circumstances are observed, you may depend upon seeing land the same day, or that following.

At the same time you will perceive, that the sea is of an iron colour, and looks as if it had small boats, with sails upon the surface[g], whilst birds resembling lories, with a red head, bill, and legs, fly around; their body is black.

As concealed shoals are often so dangerous to the navigator, I think I may pronounce you may sail in perfect safety at the distance of a league from the most suspicious parts of this whole coast.

If the discoverer should first put into port in N. L. 55. 17. he will find an inlet[h], which hath good soundings in all parts of it towards the N. and perhaps the best point[i] of the whole coast, if the ship keeps at the distance of three leagues from it.

[f] Lobos Marinos,  perhaps Seals.
[g] Unas aguas malas de color morado, que paracen unos barquichuelos, con belas latinas.
[h] Una entrada.
[i] The Journalist does not any further explain why *best.*

| 1775. Day *of* *the* Month | Latitude *by* reckoning | Latitude *by* observation | W. Long. *from* San Blas | Variation *of the* Needle | Dist. *from* *the* coast *of* America |
|---|---|---|---|---|---|
| March 1 | | | | | |
| 4 | | | | | |
| 5 | | | | | |
| 6 | | | | | |
| 7 | | | | | |
| 8 | | | | | |
| 9 | | | | | |
| 10 | | | | | |
| 11 | | | | | |
| 12 | | | | | |
| 13 | | | | | |
| 14 | | | | | |
| 15 | | | | | |
| 16 | | 21  25 | | | |
| 17 | | | | | 2 |
| 18 | | | | | 1 |
| 19 | | | | | 2 |
| 20 | | 21  34 | | 4  30* | 2 |
| 21 | | 21  39 | | * | 2 |
| 22 | | 21  43 | | * | 1 |
| 23 | | 21  47 | | | 2 |
| 24 | | 21  14 | | | 3 |
| 25 | 21  36 | 21  34 | 1  20 | | 38 |
| 26 | 20  15 | 20  10 | 1  59 | | 48 |
| 27 | 19  51 | 19  49 | 3   2 | 5 | 73 |
| 28 | 19  25 | 19  17 | 4  10 | | 79 |
| 29 | 19  23 | 19   4 | 5   1 | | 86 |
| 30 | 18  56 | 18  42 | 5  37 | | 100 |
| 31 | 18  42 | 18  33 | 5  37 | | 104 |

| 1775. Day *of* the Month | Latitude *by* reckoning | Latitude *by* observation | W. Long. *from* San Blas | Variation *of the* Needle | Dist. *from* the coast *of* America |
|---|---|---|---|---|---|
| April 1 | 18 36 | 18 33 | 5 37 | 5 | 104 |
| 2 | 18 35 | 18 33 | 5 48 | 5 13* | 107 |
| 3 | 18 56 | 18 48 | 5 27 | * | 102 |
| 4 | 18 36 | 18 30 | 6 8 | | 108 |
| 5 | 18 25 | 18 15 | 6 37 | | 117 |
| 6 | 18 2 | 17 48 | 7 31½ | | 132 |
| 7 | 17 48 | 17 43 | 8 36 | | 140 |
| 8 | 17 42 | 17 42 | 9 28 | | 148 |
| 9 | 17 43 | 17 45 | 10 22½ | | 155 |
| 10 | 17 42 | 17 35 | 11 8 | | 165 |
| 11 | 17 47 | 17 48 | 12 42 | 6 | 166 |
| 12 | 17 54 | 17 44 | 12 22½ | | 176 |
| 13 | 17 49 | 17 44 | 13 54 | | 181 |
| 14 | 17 55 | 17 47 | 14 39 | | 186 |
| 15 | 18 28 | 18 20 | 15 35 | | 186 |
| 16 | 19 6 | | 16 24½ | | 190 |
| 17 | 19 51 | 19 50 | 17 25½ | | 201 |
| 18 | 20 33 | 20 19 | 18 16½ | | 206 |
| 19 | 20 42 | 20 37 | 18 50½ | | 209 |
| 20 | 20 53 | | 19 14 | | 210 |
| 21 | 21 8 | | 20 47 | | 211 |
| 22 | 21 16 | 21 4 | 21 34½ | | 222 |
| 23 | 21 24 | 21 21 | 22 15 | | 232 |
| 24 | 21 55 | 21 47 | 23 13 | | 248 |
| 25 | 23 31 | 22 32 | 23 8 | | 259 |
| 26 | 23 20 | 23 22 | 24 13 | | 277 |
| 27 | 24 8 | 24 14 | 24 58 | | 284 |
| 28 | 24 48 | 24 50 | 25 32 | | 294 |
| 29 | 25 25 | 25 17 | 25 30 | | 300 |
| 30 | 26 3 | 25 57 | 26 22 | 7 | |

| 1775. Day *of the* Month | Latitude *by* reckoning | Latitude *by* observation | W. Long. *from* San Blas | Variation *of the* Needle | Dist. *from the* coast *of* America |
|---|---|---|---|---|---|
| May 1 | 26 29 | 26 31 | 27 07 | 7 | 302 |
| 2 | 26 45 | 26 44 | 27 19 | | 303 |
| 3 | 26 55 | 26 50 | 27 31 | | 303 |
| 4 | 27 39 | 27 30 | 28 18 | | 304 |
| 5 | 28 39 | 28 37 | 28 12 | 8 | 295 |
| 6 | 29 30 | | 29 15 | | 281 |
| 7 | 30 9 | | 30 14 | | 284 |
| 8 | 30 19 | | 30 54 | | 284 |
| 9 | 30 36 | 30 45 | 31 41 | | 291 |
| 10 | 31 18 | | 32 15 | | 297 |
| 11 | 32 12 | 32 10 | 32 50 | | 294 |
| 12 | 33 13 | 33 15 | 32 45 | | 280 |
| 13 | 33 57 | 34 3 | 31 56 | | 261 |
| 14 | 34 29 | 34 35 | 30 50 | | 239 |
| 15 | 34 26 | 34 30 | 30 12 | | 231 |
| 16 | 34 46 | 34 54 | 31 6 | | 238 |
| 17 | 34 50 | 34 50 | 31 82 | | 240 |
| 18 | 34 49 | 34 49 | 31 17 | | 240 |
| 19 | 35 46 | 35 45 | 30 20 | | 220 |
| 20 | 36 42 | 36 45 | 28 42 | 9 | 184 |
| 21 | 37 6 | 37 1 | 27 46 | | 167 |
| 22 | 37 42 | 37 46 | 28 41 | | 178 |
| 23 | 38 9 | 38 8 | 29 33 | | 185 |
| 24 | 37 48 | 37 46 | 29 10 | | 183 |
| 25 | 37 29 | 37 26 | 29 3 | | 184 |
| 26 | 37 14 | 37 11 | 28 51 | | 179 |
| 27 | 37 6 | | 29 12 | | 186 |
| 28 | 37 10 | | 29 3 | | 185 |
| 29 | 37 48 | 37 25 | 28 15½ | | 174 |
| 30 | 37 47 | 37 45 | 27 21 | | 156 |
| 31 | 37 59 | | 26 35 | 10 | 145 |

| 1775.<br>Day *of*<br>*the* Month | Latitude<br>*by*<br>reckoning | Latitude<br>*by*<br>observation | W. Long.<br>*from*<br>San Blas | Variation<br>*of the*<br>Needle | Dist. *from*<br>*the* coast *of*<br>America |
|---|---|---|---|---|---|
| June 1 | 38 21 | 38 14 | 26 12 | 10 | 128 |
| 2 | 39  3 |  | 25 26 | 12 | 122 |
| 3 | 39 46 | 39 51 | 24 38 |  | 107 |
| 4 | 40 13 |  | 23 55 | 13 30 | 89 |
| 5 | 41 11 | 41 22 | 22 58 |  | 70 |
| 6 | 41 41 | 41 37 | 21 15 |  | 42 |
| 7 | 41 49 | 41 30 | 20 19 | 14 | 33 |
| 8 | 49 59 | 41 14 | 13 13 | 14 30 |  |
| 9 | 41 25 |  | 19  4 |  |  |
| 10 |  |  |  |  |  |
| 11 |  |  |  |  |  |
| 12 |  |  |  |  |  |
| 13 |  |  |  |  |  |
| 14 |  |  |  |  |  |
| 15 |  | 41 17 |  |  |  |
| 16 |  |  |  |  |  |
| 17 |  | 41  7 |  |  |  |
| 18 |  | 41  7 | 19  4 |  |  |
| 19 |  | 40 59 | 19 21 |  |  |
| 20 |  | 40 53 | 19 41 | 14 | 12 |
| 21 | 40 59 | 40  7 | 20 56 |  | 31 |
| 22 | 40 25 | 40 | 21 41 |  | 48 |
| 23 | 40  2 |  | 23  1 |  | 67 |
| 24 | 39 45 | 39 23 | 24  7 |  | 85 |
| 25 | 39 24 | 39 20 | 25 40 | 13 | 106 |
| 26 | 39 21 | 39 21 | 26 40 |  | 121 |
| 27 | 39 22 |  | 26 30 |  | 113 |
| 28 | 39 51 |  | 26 45 |  | 118 |
| 29 | 33 43 |  | 26 25 |  | 107 |
| 30 | 40 26 | 40 16 | 26 |  |  |

| 1775.<br>Day *of*<br>*the* Month | Latitude<br>*by*<br>reckoning | Latitude<br>*by*<br>observation | W. Long.<br>*from*<br>San Blas | Variation<br>*of the*<br>Needle | Dist. *from*<br>*the* coast *of*<br>America |
|---|---|---|---|---|---|
| July 1 | 41 2 | 41 1 | 26 14 | 13 | 100 |
| 2 | 47 17 | 42 15 | 26 49 | 14 | 90 |
| 3 | 43 25 | 43 24 | 26 50 | | 70 |
| 4 | 44 21 | | 26 30½ | | 57 |
| 5 | 44 27 | | 26 10 | 15 | 47 |
| 6 | 44 24 | | 25 47 | | 32 |
| 7 | 46 10 | | 26 6 | 16 | 26 |
| 8 | 46 59 | 47 3 | 25 47 | | 12 |
| 9 | 47 44 | 47 37 | 24 20 | | |
| 10 | 47 45 | 47 35 | 23 28½ | 17 | |
| 11 | 48 32 | 48 26 | 22 17 | | 10 |
| 12 | 48 1 | 47 39 | 21 53 | | 6 |
| 13 | 47 41 | 47 28 | 21 34 | | 2 |
| 14 | 47 24 | 47 20 | 21 19 | | |
| 15 | 47 23 | 47 7 | 21 40 | 17 30 | 9 |
| 16 | 47 20 | 47 13 | 22 3 | | 17 |
| 17 | 47 17 | 47 9 | 22 22 | 17 | 18 |
| 18 | 47 3 | 46 32 | 23 32 | 16* | 35 |
| 19 | 46 34 | 46 26 | 24 28 | | 50 |
| 20 | 46 18 | 46 17 | 25 29 | | 61 |
| 21 | 46 6 | 45 57 | 27 5 | 15 | 82 |
| 22 | 45 50 | 45 44 | 28 18 | | 100 |
| 23 | 45 44 | 45 41 | 29 24 | | 115 |
| 24 | 45 51 | 45 52 | 30 32 | | 124 |
| 25 | 46 4 | 46 9 | 29 59 | | 120 |
| 26 | 46 34 | 46 32 | 29 52 | | 199 |
| 27 | 47 6 | 47 5 | 29 19 | 16* | 117 |
| 28 | 47 45 | 47 40 | 29 41 | | 103 |
| 29 | 48 10 | 47 50 | 28 44 | | 92 |
| 30 | 47 21 | 47 21 | 29 32 | | 102 |
| 31 | 46 55 | | 30 9 | | 117 |

| 1775.<br>Day *of*<br>*the* Month | Latitude<br>*by*<br>reckoning | Latitude<br>*by*<br>observation | W. Long.<br>*from*<br>San Blas | Variation<br>*of the*<br>Needle | Dist. *from*<br>*the* coast *of*<br>America |
|---|---|---|---|---|---|
| Aug.  1 | 46  34 |        | 30  56 | 16  | 131 |
| 2 | 46  45 | 46  40 | 31  52 |     | 141 |
| 3 | 46  40 | 46  35 | 32  46 |     | 157 |
| 4 | 46  29 | 46  16 | 33  39 |     | 157 |
| 5 | 46  47 | 46  47 | 34   5 |     | 171 |
| 6 | 47  49 | 47  50 | 34   6 |     | 164 |
| 7 | 48  26 | 48  24 | 34  12 |     | 159 |
| 8 | 48  39 |        | 34   7 | 17* | 156 |
| 9 | 49  11 | 49   9 | 34   7 |     | 154 |
| 10 | 50  18 |        | 34  54 | 18  | 160 |
| 11 | 51  24 | 51  34 | 34  58 |     | 159 |
| 12 | 52  18 | 52  27 | 35     | 19  | 158 |
| 13 | 53  39 | 53  54 | 35  26 |     | 161 |
| 14 | 54  58 | 55   4 | 36   7 |     | 166 |
| 15 | 55  53 | 56   8 | 35  47 |     | 154 |
| 16 | 56  43 | 56  44 | 35  15 |     | 4 |
| 17 | 56  54 | 57   2 | 35  27 |     | ⅓ |
| 18 | 57  21 |        | 35  27 |     |   |
| 19 |        |        |        |     |   |
| 20 |        |        |        |     |   |
| 21 |        |        |        |     | ⅓ |
| 22 | 57  55 | 57  57 | 38   2 | 20  |   |
| 23 | 57  10 | 57   8 | 35  50 | 22* | 2 |
| 24 | 56   1 |        | 33  46 | 24* | 1 |
| 25 | 55  17 | 55  17 | 33  24 |     |   |
| 26 | 56   6 | 55   6 | 33  22 | 24  |   |
| 27 |        |        |        |     |   |
| 28 | 55  36 |        | 34  39 | 23* | 2 |
| 29 | 55  55 | 55  55 | 34  32 |     | ⅓ |
| 30 | 56  21 |        | 35     |     | ⅓ |
| 31 | 56  41 | 56  47 | 35  32 |     | ½ |

| 1775.<br>Day *of*<br>*the* Month | Latitude<br>*by*<br>reckoning | Latitude<br>*by*<br>observation | W. Long.<br>*from*<br>San Blas | Variation<br>*of the*<br>Needle | Dist. *from*<br>*the* coast *of*<br>America |
|---|---|---|---|---|---|
| Sept. 1 | 56 31 | | 16 10 | 23 | 10 |
| 2 | 56 5 | 56 3 | 36 22 | 23 30 | 17 |
| 3 | 55 45 | 55 47 | 36 39 | 23 | 21 |
| 4 | 55 28 | | 36 33 | | 22 |
| 5 | 55 8 | 55 7 | 37 5 | | 26 |
| 6 | 54 40 | 54 42 | 36 27 | 22 | 20 |
| 7 | 54 53 | | 36 56 | 23 | 26 |
| 8 | 55 4 | | 36 56 | | 26 |
| 9 | 54 39 | 54 32 | 35 22 | 21 | 7 |
| 10 | 54 4 | 54 6 | 34 6 | | 6 |
| 11 | 53 54 | 53 52 | 32 19 | 20 | 8 |
| 12 | 52 58 | | 31 5 | | 8 |
| 13 | 52 11 | 52 9 | 30 | | 9 |
| 14 | 51 14 | 51 16 | 29 35 | | 9 |
| 15 | 50 4 | 50 12 | 27 2 | | 9 |
| 16 | 49 23 | 49 21 | 25 38 | | 9 |
| 17 | 48 51 | 48 53 | 24 35 | | 7 |
| 18 | 48 37 | 48 33 | 23 40 | 19 | 6 |
| 19 | 47 50 | 47 49 | 23 10 | | ½ |
| 20 | 47 11 | 47 12 | 22 33 | | ½ |
| 21 | 46 21 | | 21 58 | | 11 |
| 22 | 46 20 | | 22 42 | | 10 |
| 23 | 45 38 | | 22 35 | | ⅓ |
| 24 | 44 47 | 44 47 | 21 12 | | ⅓ |
| 25 | 44 17 | 44 19 | 21 2 | 18 | ½ |
| 26 | 43 15 | 43 16 | 21 20 | 17 | 10 |
| 27 | 42 37 | | 21 41 | | 12 |
| 28 | 42 37 | | 21 41 | | 10 |
| 29 | 41 1 | 40 54 | 21 41 | | ½ |
| 30 | 39 38 | 39 42 | 21 11 | 16 | ½ |

| 1775.<br>Day *of*<br>*the* Month | Latitude<br>*by*<br>reckoning | Latitude<br>*by*<br>observation | W. Long.<br>*from*<br>San Blas | Variation<br>*of the*<br>Needle | Dist. *from*<br>*the* coast *of*<br>America |
|---|---|---|---|---|---|
| Oct.   1 | 39  17 | 39  15 | 20  26 | 16 | ½ |
| 2 | 38  49 | 38  49 | 19   5 | 16 | ½ |
| 3 | 38  16 | 38  16 | 19   2 | 16 | |
| 4 | 38  16 | 38  16 | 19  22 | 16 | |
| 5 | 37  54 | 37  53 | 19  24 | 15 | 3 |
| 6 | 37  45 | 37  43 | 19   4 | 15 | 1 |
| 7 | 36  43 | 36  42 | 18  47 | 14 | |
| 8 | 36  46 | | 17  17 | 14 | |

| 1775.<br>Day *of*<br>*the* Month | Latitude<br>*by*<br>reckoning | Latitude<br>*by*<br>observation | W. Long.<br>*from*<br>San Blas | Variation<br>*of the*<br>Needle | Dist. *from*<br>*the* coast *of*<br>America |
|---|---|---|---|---|---|
| Nov. 2 | 36 44 | 36 42 | 17 5 | 14 | 7 |
| 3 | 36 28 | | 17 27 | 13 | 8 |
| 4 | 36 6 | 36 11 | 17 42 | 12 | 8 |
| 5 | 34 41 | 34 36 | 17 25 | 11 | 23 |
| 6 | 32 50 | 32 48 | 16 58 | 10 | 45 |
| 7 | 30 56 | 30 57 | 16 2 | 9 | 48 |
| 8 | 29 32 | | 15 18 | 8 | 46 |
| 9 | 28 52 | | 14 45 | 7 | 45 |
| 10 | 28 21 | 27 52 | 14 13 | 7 | 42 |
| 11 | 27 16 | 27 8 | 13 26 | 7 | 35 |
| 12 | 26 16 | 26 12 | 12 13 | 7 | 24 |
| 13 | 25 18 | 25 16 | 10 46 | 6 | 38 |
| 14 | 24 53 | 24 37 | 8 58 | 6 | 6 |
| 15 | 24 15 | 24 1 | 6 56 | 6 | 10 |
| 16 | 23 2 | 23 | 5 25 | 5 | 1½ |
| 17 | 22 20 | 22 22 | 4 3 | 5 | 40 |
| 18 | 21 54 | 21 53 | 2 38 | | 10 |
| 19 | 21 45 | 21 44 | 0 46 | 5 | 3 |
| 20 | 21 36 | 21 34 | 0 2 | 5 | |

35
30
25
20
15
10
5
60
C. S.t Elias
Highest Latitude of the Voyage
P.ta de los Remedios
P.ta Guadalupe & M. S. Jacinto
C. del Engaño
Tchirikow's Land
Land of Vulcanos
P.to Bucarely
C. S.t Augustine
S. Carlos
FOU-SANG of the Chinese, according to Mr de Guignes.
NORTH AMERICA
N.B. The places mark'd in Roman Characters are those only whose Longitude & Latitude have been settled by this Voyage
60
55
55
Cook's Harbour 1778
NORTH PART
I. de Dolores
50
50
C. Mezari
45
45
C. Blanco
C. Mendocin
P.to de la Trinidad
R. de las Tortolas
NEW
P.ta de Arenas
R. de los dolores
P.to de la Bodega
S.t Francis Drake's Harb. 1578
el Cordon
ALBION
Monterey
P.ta de la Conception
OF THE
40
40
GREAT SEA
C. Blanco
CALIFORNIA
MAR. VERMEJO
Meridian of San Blas 106 D. 57 M. from Paris.
104 D. 32 M. from London.
Deduced from the Observations made at San Joset in 1769, by L'Abbé Chappe d'Auteroche.
MEXICO
35
35
Guadalupe
Morro Hermoso
30
30
C. N.ra S.ra de las Nieves
25
25
North Tropic
Shebrocks I.
San Joset
C. San Lucas
NEW
SAN BLAS
GALICIA
or PACIFIC OCEAN
las Tres Marias
C. de Corientes
20
Socorro.
20
Longitude West from San Blas
35
30
25
20
15
10
5

# ADDENDA *to* p. 18, note [*a*]

Having admitted in this note, that I do not thoroughly understand the journalist's description, it is right to add, that the manner mentioned of disfiguring the face, is illustrated by a wooden masque in Sir Ashton Lever's Museum, brought from no distant latitude on this same coast of America.

P. 14. Fifth line from the bottom.

I am informed by a gentleman long resident at Cadiz, that *espiare* signifies *to warp* as well as to *spy*; and I rather conceive that in this passage it should have been so translated.


FINIS.

[57] A DUTCH WHALER OFF THE COAST OF GREENLAND.
From an engraving in Groenewegen, *Hollandse Scheepen,* Amsterdam, 1789, in the Clark Collection, Massachusetts Institute of Technology.

# INDEX & NOTES

[126] SHIP "MARIA," OF NEW BEDFORD, BUILT AT
PEMBROKE, MASS., IN 1782.
The oldest whaler in the United States in 1853.
From a wood engraving in the Allan Forbes Collection.

# NOTES

## PAGE 3  iii/471*

Archivo of Simanca. The Spanish title is, Archivo General de Simancas; loosely, in English, the archives of Simancas.

Many of the archives were carried to Paris during the Napoleonic wars, but some were returned later. The government has made them now accessible.

## Robertson's History of America.

This work was first published in 1777 (2 vols., 4to). Notwithstanding the statement in the note on page 3, Robertson obtained, through the influence of friends, much valuable information from Spanish archives. Robertson is reckoned among the best British historical writers, but it is said of him that he was too apt to be satisfied with secondary and commonplace authorities. His researches have been surpassed, or corrected and amplified, by Prescott, in regard to America.

## PAGE 4  *472/iv

Venegas's History of California. The title-page of the original edition reads: Noticia de la California, y de su Conquista Temporal, y Espiritual hasta el Tiempo Presente. Sacada de la historia manuscrita, formada en Mexico año de 1739. por el Padre Miguèl Venegas, de la Compañia de Jesus; y de Otras Noticias, y Relaciones antiguas, y modernas. Anadida de Algunas Mapas Particulares, y uno general de la America Septentrional, Asia Oriental, y Mar del Sùr intermedio, formados sobre las Memorias mas recientes, y exactas, que se publìcan juntamente. Dedicada Al Rey N.tro Señor por la provincia de Nueva-España, de la Compañia de Jesus. Tomo Primero [Segundo y Tercero]. Con Licencia. En Madrid: En la Imprenta de la Viuda de Manuel Fernandez, y del Supremo Consejo de la Inquisicion. Año de M.D.CCLVII.

79

The title-page of the Spanish edition of Venegas's History of California is here printed in full, and with all its inaccuracies and eccentricities, with the exception of lines or single words set in capitals. Printers and authors make changes, seemingly for no better reason than to amend the original to conform to their ideas of what it should be, whether right or wrong. Barrington's error — 1747, instead of 1757 — in the date of publication of Venegas is easily accounted for. The English translation of Venegas was published in London in 1759, in two volumes, and is a miserable piece of work. The reader will look therein in vain for the part concerning the Northwest Passage; it is omitted. It will be noted that the quotation on page 4 is from the Spanish edition. Greenhow, in his History of Oregon and California (Boston, 1844), says of Venegas: —

This work, though usually attributed to Venegas, is doubtless chiefly due to the labors of Father Andres Marcos Burriel. The portions relating to the proceedings of the Jesuits in California are highly interesting, and bear every internal mark of truth and authenticity. The observations on the policy of the Spanish government towards its American possessions are replete with wisdom, and indicate more liberality, as well as boldness, on the part of the authors, than could have been reasonably expected, considering the circumstances under which they were written and published.

## PAGE 5   v/473*

Chappe Dauteroche = Jean Chappe d'Auteroche.

This eminent French astronomer was sent by l'Académie des Sciences to California in 1769 to observe the transit of Venus, but he died at San José del Cabo shortly after his arrival. His Voyage de la Californie was published in 1772, and the English translation thereof in 1778. The map in the first edition of Maurelle's Journal was deduced from observations made by him at San José del Cabo.

## PAGE 6   *474/vi

St. Lewis de Sacatecas = San Luis de Zacatecas.

Guanacabelica = Huancavelica. A department and one of the richest cities of Perú.

Gage's Survey of the West Indies. The general title of this work reads: A New Survey of the West-India's; or the English American, his Travail by Sea and Land: containing a Journal of Three hundred Miles within the main Land of America. By . . . Thomas Gage, Preacher.

The first edition of this work appeared in 1648. Gage, an English Catholic missionary to Spanish America, on his return to England embraced Protestantism, and his work, by showing the defenseless condition of the Spanish possessions, led to privateering expeditions against them. Southey the poet wrote in his copy, —

Gage was a great scoundrel, and has transcribed part of his book from an old translation of Gomara [Francisco López de Gómara (1510–1559), author of Historia General de las Indias]. We may trust him, however, for Jamaica, where he was killed when the conquest of that island was made. There are many curious things in the book, and the author, like others of his stamp, may be believed in those cases where he had no motives for telling a lie.

Don Alzate = José Antonio Alzate y Ramírez, a noted Mexican scientist, and the author and translator of numerous works.

## Page 7   vii/475*

Charts made by Maurelle on the Sonora.

As to the nine charts made by Maurelle, and referred to so often in the Journal, Bancroft (History of the Northwest Coast, vol. i, p. 166) states that they have unfortunately never been published, and are not even known to exist in manuscript.

Register ship. Sp., registro, a single vessel from the Indies, with goods registered in port.

## Page 8   *476/viii

Don Juan Peres (Pérez), the piloto of the Santiago, under Heceta, in the present expedition, was, like Serra, a Majorcan.

Pérez held the rank of alférez (ensign) de fragata in the royal navy, and had been piloto, or sailing-master, in the Manila service. His MS. documents, etc., are much quoted by historians.

In " la santa expedición " (sacred expedition) of Gálvez, for the spiritual conquest of Nueva California, in 1769, Pérez was the commander of the San Antonio (otherwise El Príncipe), carrying supplies for the foundation of the new Franciscan establishments at San Diego and Monterey, and was the first to reach those ports. Portolá, at the same time, going by land to these ports, missing Monterey, accidentally discovered the Bay of San Francisco. In the first Bucareli expedition north of California, in 1774, Pérez, with orders to follow the coast northward of 60°, sailed from San Blas on January 24th, in command of the Santiago (otherwise Nueva Galicia), carrying Serra and officials to San Diego, where they arrived on March 13th. The coast was surveyed to 55°, but no landing was anywhere made, and on July 22d the return voyage was begun. Monterey was reached on August 27th, and San Blas on November 3d. In the second expedition sent northward of California by Bucareli,—that of 1775, in which De la Bodega y Quadra was in command of the Sonora, and Maurelle, the author of this Journal, was piloto,— Pérez was the piloto primero of Heceta, comandante of the expedition, in the Santiago. Latitude 49° was reached by the Santiago on August 11th,—they had left San Blas on March 16th,— when they returned south. Monterey was reached on August 29th, where the scurvy-stricken members of the crew were landed, and all hospitably entertained by the padres of the Mission of San Carlos Borromeo. The Santiago with Heceta and Pérez was at Monterey when the Sonora with De la Bodega and Maurelle arrived there on October 7th, and both sailed together for San Blas on November 1st, arriving on the 20th. Pérez died on the second day out, in sight of Misión San Carlos. He was a friend of the Padre Presidente Junípero Serra.

## Attempts of the English to discover a N.W. Passage.

Alarm was undoubtedly felt by the Spaniards that the English might transfer the scene of their operations to the coast of California should they discover a Northwest Passage. The attempts of Arthur Dobbs, and especially the publication in 1748 of Ellis's Voyage, led to the printing of an appendix relating thereto in Venegas's Noticia de California, but omitted from the English translation, as stated in the note to page 4 (p. 80, ante). Ellis's title-page is reprinted below.

A Voyage to Hudson's Bay, by the Dobbs Galley and California, in 1746 and 1747, for Discovering a North West Passage; with An Accurate Survey of the Coast, and a short Natural History of the Country. Together with A Fair View of the Facts and Arguments from which the future finding of such a Passage is rendered possible. By Henry Ellis, Gent. Agent for the Proprietors in the said Expedition. To which is prefixed, An Historical Account of the Attempts hitherto made for the finding a Passage that Way to the East-Indies. Illustrated with proper cuts, and a new and correct Chart of Hudson's-Bay, with the countries adjacent. London: Printed for H. Whitridge, at the Royal Exchange. M.DCC.XLVIII.

## PAGE 9    ix/477*

## Captain James Cook. Voyage to the Northwest Coast.

This famous English navigator was, like Drake, of obscure parentage, his father being a farm-laborer. He was born in Yorkshire in 1728. Entering the royal navy in 1755 as a volunteer, he soon distinguished himself, and promotion followed recognition of his merits as a navigator of the first order. He discovered the Sandwich Islands on January 18, 1778, proceeding thence to the Northwest Coast, sighting it just north of California, and, sailing northward, surveyed the whole coast, including Nootka Sound, Alaska, the Aleutian Islands, and Bering's Strait, until the ice-barrier prevented farther progress, resulting in his bitter disappointment in not finding a Northwest Passage. Then surveying the northeast coast of Asia, he returned to the Sandwich Islands, where he was killed by the natives on the island of Hawaii, February 13, 1779. The title-page of his voyages follows.

A Voyage to the Pacific Ocean. Undertaken by the command of His Majesty, for Making Discoveries in the Northern Hemisphere, To determine the position and extent of the west side of North America; its Distance from Asia; and the practicability of a northern passage to Europe. Performed under the direction of Captains Cook, Clerke, and Gore, in His Majesty's ships the Resolution and Discovery, in the Years 1776, 1777, 1778, 1779, and 1780. Vol. I. and II. by Captain James Cook, F. R. S. Vol. III. by Captain James King, LL. D. and F. R. S. Illustrated with Maps and Charts [etc.] . . . Published by Order of the Lords Commissioners of the Admiralty. . . . London: Printed . . . For G. Nicol, . . . MDCCLXXXIV.

## Dr. Halley. Variation of the needle.

Dr. Edmund Halley (1656–1742), the celebrated English astronomer, better remembered in connection with the comet which bears his name, published, in 1701, the work entitled A General Chart Showing the Variation of the Needle.

## San Blas.     PAGE 11    3/471

This port, so intimately associated with the early history of the Californias and the Missions, owed its importance to its naval establishment. The town is built on a rock 150 feet high, which rises out of a low swampy plain. The Viceroy Bucareli, in 1773, had determined to abandon the port, but Junípero Serra, who visited him in that year, represented to him, says Forbes in his History of California, that this was the only place from which a communication could be kept up with California, and so fully impressed him with the importance of the new Missions, that he not only consented to continue the establishment, but also ordered a frigate (the Santiago) to be finished for the purpose of exploring the coast of Nueva California.

### The Bells of San Blas

THE LAST POEM WRITTEN BY LONGFELLOW — MARCH 15, 1882

What say the Bells of San Blas
To the ships that southward pass
    From the harbor of Mazatlán ?
To them it is nothing more
Than the sound of surf on the shore,—
    Nothing more to master or man.

But to me, a dreamer of dreams,
To whom what is and what seems
    Are often one and the same,—
The Bells of San Blas to me
Have a strange, wild melody,
    And are something more than a name.

For bells are the voice of the church ;
They have tones that touch and search
    The hearts of young and old ;
One sound to all, yet each
Lends a meaning to their speech,
    And the meaning is manifold.

They are a voice of the Past,
Of an age that is fading fast,
    Of a power austere and grand,
When the flag of Spain unfurled
Its folds o'er this western world,
    And the Priest was lord of the land.

The chapel that once looked down
On the little seaport town
    Has crumbled into the dust ;
And on oaken beams below
The bells swing to and fro,
    And are green with mold and rust.

"Is, then, the old faith dead,"
They say, "and in its stead
    Is some new faith proclaimed,
That we are forced to remain
Naked to sun and rain,
    Unsheltered and ashamed ?

"Once, in our tower aloof,
We rang over wall and roof
    Our warnings and our complaints ;
And round about us there
The white doves filled the air,
    Like the white souls of the saints.

"The saints !  Ah, have they grown
Forgetful of their own ?
    Are they asleep, or dead,
That open to the sky
Their ruined Missions lie,
    No longer tenanted ?

"Oh, bring us back once more
The vanished days of yore,
    When the world with faith was filled ;
Bring back the fervid zeal,
The hearts of fire and steel,
    The hands that believe and build.

"Then from our tower again
We will send over land and main
    Our voices of command,
Like exiled kings who return
To their thrones, and the people learn
    That the Priest is lord of the land !"

    O Bells of San Blas, in vain
    Ye call back the Past again ;
       The Past is deaf to your prayer !
    Out of the shadows of night
    The world rolls into light ;
       It is daybreak everywhere.

### Fero = Ferro, the Spanish Hierro.

The most southwestern of the Canary Islands. The promontory on its west coast, now called Dehesa, was formerly famous as the point through which the universal first meridian was drawn. It is 17° 40′ west of Greenwich.

### Mons. Bellin's charts.

Carte réduite de l'Océan septentrional, compris entre l'Asie et l'Amérique, suivant les Découvertes faites par les Russes. Par N. Bellin. Paris, 1766.

## PAGE 13  5/473

### Don Antonio Maria Bucareli and Ursua.

The most popular and the most successful of the viceroys of Nueva España, El Bailio Frey Don Antonio María Bucareli y Ursúa was born at Seville, January 24, 1717, and died at Mexico, April 9, 1779. As his paternal surname indicates, his ancestors on that side were of Italian origin, and on both sides the families from which he sprang were illustrious, and he nobly upheld the best qualities of the Latin race. Viceroy from 1771 until his death, he was the friend of Serra and of the Missions, the indefatigable promoter of shipbuilding and navigation and discovery on the Californian and Northwest coasts.

### His Majesty   Charles III of Spain.

Don Carlos III, one of the Bourbon kings of Spain, was born January 20, 1716; on February 27, 1767, issued a mandate for the expulsion of the Jesuits from his dominions, which was confirmed by the pragmatic sanction of April 2d; he was, at various times, at war with England, France, and the Moors; died at Madrid, December 14, 1788.

### Don Bruno Heceta, comandante of the fragata Santiago.

Heceta was a teniente de navío, or lieutenant in the royal navy, and was the comandante of this the second expedition sent out by Bucareli to survey the coast northward of California. Maurelle, in his Journal, has recorded the movements of Heceta in the Santiago until she was lost sight of by the Sonora on July 31st. An extract from the report of Heceta, showing further movements, will be found farther along in this note. The Santiago had reached latitude 49° on August 11th, when, the crew being stricken with scurvy, Heceta headed southward, surveying, as recorded in the report, the coast of the continent. He intended to enter the new port of San Francisco, but, owing to the fogs, he could not find the entrance, and Monterey was reached on August 29th. His scurvy-stricken crew being left in the sympathetic charge of the good padres at San Carlos Borromeo, Heceta planned to assist Ayala in the survey of the bay and harbor of San Francisco, a land party for that purpose, promised by Rivera, not having been sent. On the 14th of September they set out, escorted by nine soldiers. Fr. Miguel de la Campa Cos, a chaplain of the Santiago (the other was Fr. Benito Sierra), and Fr. Francisco Palou were sent by Junípero Serra as chaplains, and to select the site for the future Mission of San Francisco. Following the route of Rivera in 1774, on the 22d they were at the beach just south of the present Cliff House. Here they found Ayala's cayuco, the dugout built on the Rio Carmelo; and, following the beach to Punto de los Lobos, ascended the hill, and on its summit, at the foot of the cross erected there by Rivera in 1774, they found two letters from Fr. Vicente de Santa María, the chaplain of the San Carlos, Ayala's paquebote. One of these letters directed the land party to go a league inland and light a fire on the beach, which would be seen by the San Carlos at her place of anchorage at the Isla de Nuestra Señora de los Ángeles in case she had not sailed for Monterey, the survey of the new port of San Francisco being finished. The other letter was simply a notification of a successful arrival and anchorage at the port. Heceta proceeded to the Punta del Cantil Blanco (literally, the point of the precipitous white cliff),—the present Fort Point,—and, the signals of the party meeting with no response, return was made to the camp which they had left on the shores of a laguna, which they named La Laguna de Nuestra Señora de la Merced (the lake of Our Mother of Mercy), on the 24th of September, and from thence proceeded to Monterey, arriving there on the 1st of October. The San Carlos had left San Francisco on September 18th, and arrived at Monterey the next day. This party of Heceta consisted of only three sailors and a carpenter, besides the padres and the military escort. On the back of a mule a small canoe was carried. How the supplies were carried, history saith not. The party accomplished nothing. The goleta Sonora arrived at Monterey on October 7th. Her stricken crew and that of the Santiago were cared for at the Mission of San Carlos Borromeo, the headquarters of the Padre Presidente Serra, and the command, again united, sailed for San Blas on November 1st, arriving on the 20th, Pérez, the piloto primero of Heceta, dying two days out from Monterey. Heceta's name does not further appear in California history. Of this second expedition, Bucareli, in letters to Don Carlos III, stated that, if not wholly disproved by this voyage, it at least has been reduced to a very slender possibility that there leads westward any passage from Hudson's Bay; he approved a recommendation by Heceta that the port of Trinidad be fortified, and wrote in the strongest terms of the courage and resourcefulness of De la Bodega y Quadra. As to Heceta and Pérez, on this voyage of the Santiago, must be credited the discovery of the mouth of the Columbia, it will be deemed proper to print, at this point in these Notes, Greenhow's translation of that part of Heceta's journal concerning the same, it being the personal narrative of Heceta. At the same time, in a measure it helps to round out the record of accomplishment of the expedition. The translation, as made by Greenhow, is not here changed in any way, although faulty in places.

*Extract from the Report of Captain Bruno Heceta, commanding the Spanish Corvette Santiago, in a Voyage along the North-West Coast of America, in 1775, containing the Particulars of his Discovery of the Mouth of the Great River, since called the Columbia.*

FROM THE ORIGINAL REPORT, PRESERVED IN THE HYDROGRAPHICAL OFFICE AT MADRID. COPIED UNDER THE SUPERVISION OF DON MARTIN FERNANDES DE NAVARATE, THE CHIEF OF THAT DEPARTMENT, WHOSE CERTIFICATE IN PROOF OF ITS AUTHENTICITY IS APPENDED TO THE COPY.

On the 17th [of August, 1775] I sailed along the coast to the 46th degree, and observed that, from the latitude of 47 degrees 4 minutes to that of 46 degrees 40 minutes, it runs in the angle of 18 degrees of the second quadrant,* and from that latitude to 46 degrees 4 minutes, in the angle of 12 degrees of the same quadrant; the soundings, the shore, the wooded character of the country, and the little islands, being the same as on the preceding days.

In the evening of this day, I discovered a large bay, to which I gave the name of *Assumption Bay*, and of which a plan will be found in this journal. Its latitude and longitude are determined according to the most exact means afforded by theory and practice.

The latitudes of the two most prominent capes of this bay, especially of the northern one, are calculated from the observations of this day. †

Having arrived opposite this bay at six in the evening, and placed the ship nearly midway between the two capes, I sounded, and found bottom in twenty-four *brazas*; ‡ the currents and eddies

---

* The card of the Spanish compass was formerly divided into four quadrants, on which the points were counted by degrees.

† In the table accompanying the report, the position of the vessel is given on the 17th of August, as in latitude of 46 degrees 17 minutes, which is within one minute of the latitude of Cape Disappointment, (the *Cape San Roque* of Heceta,) the northern point, at the entrance of the Columbia; the longitude is made 15 degrees 38 minutes west of Cape San Lucas, the southern extremity of California, which is about a degree and a half too far west, yet remarkably near the truth, considering that the Spanish navigator was obliged to depend entirely on the dead reckoning for his longitudes.

‡ The Spanish *braza*, or fathom, contains six Spanish feet, nearly equal to five feet nine inches English.

were so strong that, notwithstanding a press of sail, it was difficult to get out clear of the northern cape, towards which the current ran, though its direction was eastward, in consequence of the tide being at flood.

These currents and eddies of the water caused me to believe that the place is the mouth of some great river, or of some passage to another sea.

Had I not been certain of the latitude of this bay, from my observations of the same day, I might easily have believed it to be the passage discovered by Juan de Fuca, in 1592, which is placed on the charts between the 47th and the 48th degrees; where I am certain that no such strait exists; because I anchored on the 14th of July midway between these two latitudes, and carefully examined every thing around.

Notwithstanding the great difference between the position of this bay and the passage mentioned by De Fuca, I have little difficulty in conceiving that they may be the same, having observed equal or greater differences in the latitudes of other capes and ports on this coast, as I shall show at its proper time; and in all cases the latitudes thus assigned are higher than the real ones.

I did not enter and anchor in this port, which in my plan I suppose to be formed by an island, notwithstanding my strong desire to do so; because, having consulted the second captain, Don Juan Perez, and the pilot, Don Christoval Revilla, they insisted that I ought not to attempt it, as, if we let go the anchor, we should not have men enough to get it up, and to attend to the other operations which would be thereby rendered necessary. Considering this, and also that, in order to reach the anchorage, I should be obliged to lower my long-boat, (the only boat that I had,) and to man it with at least fourteen of the crew, as I could not manage with fewer, and also that it was then late in the day, I resolved to put out; and at the distance of three or four leagues I lay to. In the course of that night, I experienced heavy currents to the south-west, which made it impossible for me to enter the bay on the following morning, as I was far to leeward.

These currents, however, convinced me that a great quantity of water rushed from this bay on the ebb of the tide.

The two capes which I name in my plan *Cape San Roque* * and *Cape Frondoso*, † lie in the angle of ten degrees of the third quadrant. They are both faced with red earth, and are of little elevation.

On the 18th, I observed *Cape Frondoso*, with another cape, to which I gave the name of *Cape Falcon*, ‡ situated in the latitude of 45 degrees 43 minutes, and they lay at the angle of 22 degrees of the third quadrant, and from the last-mentioned cape I traced the coast running in the angle of five degrees of the second quadrant.

This land is mountainous, but not very high, nor so well wooded as that lying between the latitudes of 48 degrees 30 minutes, and 46 degrees.

On sounding, I found great differences: at the distance of 7 leagues, I got bottom at 84 *brazas*; and nearer the coast, I sometimes found no bottom; from which I am inclined to believe that there are reefs or shoals on these coasts, which is also shown by the color of the water. In some places, the coast presents a beach, in others it is rocky.

A flat-topped mountain, which I named *The Table*, § will enable any navigator to know the position of *Cape Falcon* without observing it; as it is in the latitude of 45 degrees 28 minutes, and may be seen at a great distance, being somewhat elevated.

| | |
|---|---|
| * Cape Disappointment. | ‡ Cape Lookout. |
| † Cape Adams. | § Charke's [Clark's] Point of View. |

Frigate (Sp., fragata) = the Santiago, or Nueva Galicia.

This vessel was built at San Blas. When Junípero Serra made his memorable visit to the Viceroy Bucareli in México in 1773, the port of San Blas was about to be abandoned, and the Santiago, then on the stocks, would probably never have been finished, had not Serra impressed upon the Viceroy the necessity of the port, and the disadvantages attending the transportation overland of Mission supplies. The Santiago, finished and ready for sea, was ordered by Bucareli on an exploring expedition northward of California, rumors of encroachments by the Russians causing anxiety in old Spain, aggravated by the fear that the English might be successful in discovering a Northwest Passage. On January 24, 1774, the Santiago, under the command of Juan Pérez, sailed from San Blas to execute her commission, with Serra as a passenger to go to Monterey, and with supplies for the northern Missions; but, says Forbes in his History of California, "Although they were bound direct to Monterey, yet, from some of those fatalities which never ceased to attend them, they were obliged to put into San Diego, where they arrived on the 13th of March. . . . The frigate afterwards pursued her voyage to Monterey, but Father Junípero chose to go overland for the purpose of visiting the other Missions.'' The arrival of the Santiago with supplies, at Monterey, on May 9th, occasioned much joy and relieved dire distress. With instructions to reach 60°, and with Padre Juan Crespi and Padre Tomás de la Peña as chaplains and diarists, Pérez in the Santiago sailed from Monterey on June 11th, surveyed the coast to the extremity of Queen Charlotte Island in latitude 55°. Heading southwards, he passed the Farallones on August 26th, and was at Monterey on the 27th; leaving there on October 9th, San Blas was reached on November 3d. Maurelle, in his Journal, having recorded the voyage of the Santiago under Heceta and Pérez, in the second expedition sent out by Bucareli in 1775, until her separation from the goleta Sonora on July 31st, and her further movements on this voyage being recorded in the notes (pp. 81, 84 et seq., ante) on Pérez and Heceta, further notice thereof is not deemed necessary here. On March 1, 1777, with Ignacio Arteaga as capitan and Francisco Castro as piloto, the Santiago left San Blas for San Francisco, and arrived on May 12th,—the first vessel to sail from a Mexican port direct to San Francisco. She sailed, on the return voyage, on May 27th, stopped at Monterey on the 28th, and left on June 8th for San Blas. Padre José Nocedal acted as the chaplain on this voyage. On June 17, 1778, with Juan Manuel de Ayala in command, Francisco Castro and Juan Bautista Aguirre as pilotos, and Padre José Nocedal as chaplain, the Santiago arrived at San Francisco, 105 days out from San Blas (March 8th); sailed on July 27th; stopped at Monterey on the 31st to discharge supplies. With Serra as a passenger for San Diego, anchor was weighed on August 25th, but contrary winds prevented sailing until September 6th, and San Diego was reached on the 15th. On June 26, 1779, the Santiago again arrived at San Francisco, with Estévan José Martínez as capitan, José Tobar as piloto, and, as chaplain, Rdo. Nicolás de Ibera, the first secular priest in Nueva California, bringing information which created consternation among the missionaries,—proposed political changes, involving the erection of a new diocese, and the jurisdiction of the Viceroy of Nueva España; leaving San Francisco on July 26th, the Santiago was nearly wrecked outside the harbor, and again off Punta de Año Nuevo; she stopped at Monterey and San Diego, remaining at the latter port till the middle of October. On October 7, 1780, the Santiago arrived at Monterey, with the same capitan and piloto as in 1779, and with a secular priest, Rdo. Miguel Dávalos, as chaplain; discharging her supplies, she immediately returned to San Blas, the supplies for the San Francisco establishment having to be carried there on muleback. Arriving at San Blas in January, 1781, the Santiago was dispatched to Perú for a cargo of quicksilver, and her subsequent history is to us unknown.

## Schooner (Sp., goleta) = the schooner or goleta Sonora, also called La Felicidad.

The measurements of this little craft, as well as her crew on this expedition, are given in an old Spanish work as '' una goleta de 18 codos de quilla y 6 de manga, tripulado con un piloto, un contramaestre, un guardián, diez marineros, un paje y un criado''; which, freely translated into English, is, a schooner of thirty-six feet keel and twelve feet beam, manned by a mate, a boatswain, a storekeeper (that is, of arms, as well as stores), ten sailors, a cabin-boy, and a servant. The depth (eight feet) is omitted in the measurement.

## Don Juan de Ayala = Don Juan Manuel de Ayala.

Ayala was born in the historic town of Osuna, Andalucía, December 27, 1745; entered the Marine Corps, September 19, 1760; commissioned alférez de fragata, October 10, 1767; alférez de navío, June 15, 1769; teniente de fragata, April 28,

[8]

1774, in which year, at Mexico, he was ordered to San Blas, where he was given command of the Sonora, and later transferred to the San Carlos, as recorded in the Journal. Ayala awaited the return of the boat which carried his demented predecessor, Manrique, back to San Blas, and on the 21st of March sailed for the new port of San Francisco. Early in April he was severely wounded in one foot when a loaded pistol, belonging to Manrique, fell on the floor of the cabin, and the active work involved in the survey of the harbor of San Francisco necessarily devolved upon his pilotos, Cañizares and Aguirre. Ayala was, however, the first commander of a vessel to pass through the Golden Gate,—the San Carlos, late in the evening of August 5, 1775. (See notes post, to page 14, on the San Carlos, and to page 58, on San Francisco.) Ayala was afterwards made teniente de navio, February, 1776, and capitan de fragata, December 21, 1782. He returned to Spain, July, 1784; was retired, at his own request, March 14, 1785, and was granted, in consideration of his services in California, full pay as capitan de fragata. He died on the 13th of December, 1797.

## Don Juan Francisco de la Bodega = Don Juan Francisco de la Bodega y Quadra (or Cuadra).

De la Bodega, like Ayala, was a teniente de fragata at the time of the sailing of the Sonora from San Blas. On the third Bucareli expedition in 1779, he was comandante of La Favorita, or Nuestra Señora de los Remedios, a vessel built in Perú, and Maurelle was segundo capitan. Cañizares and Aguirre were pilotos, as they had been, in 1775, on the San Carlos. Rdo. Cristóbal Díaz, a secular priest from Lima, was chaplain. Don Bruno Heceta (see note ante, page 84), who commanded the Santiago in 1775, was at first named as comandante of the expedition and also of La Princesa, or Nuestra Señora del Rosario, a vessel built at San Blas, but subsequently, and before sailing, the command was given to Don Ignacio de Arteaga, although De la Bodega, in consideration of former services, was entitled thereto. Fernando Quirós y Miranda was segundo capitan of La Princesa, and José Camacho and Juan Pantoja y Arriaga were pilotos. The Padres Juan García Riobó and Matias Noriega were chaplains. The vessels sailed from San Blas on February 11, 1779, under orders to reach 70° N. They attained about 60°, but, being attacked by scurvy, Arteaga ordered a return, against the protests of De la Bodega and Maurelle, for which he is severely criticised by historians. Drakes Bay was surveyed on the way south. La Favorita entered the port of San Francisco on the 14th of September, and La Princesa on the 15th, and an enthusiastic reception was accorded the officers and crews. The Padre Presidente Serra, then at Monterey, was invited by the officers of the expedition to come to San Francisco, but, declining, De la Bodega and Padre Palóu, with others, set out to visit him at the Misión San Carlos. Serra, in the mean time, had changed his mind, and he met his visitors at the Misión Santa Clara. He had walked all the way from Monterey, and refused the offer of the surgeon of the expedition to treat his ulcerated leg. A short time after the return of De la Bodega and party, with Serra, to San Francisco, a courier arrived overland with tidings of the death of Bucareli, and of the declaration of war by Spain against England. Dreading hostilities on the high seas, La Princesa and La Favorita sailed hastily for San Blas on October 30th, arriving there on November 21st. De la Bodega, later, was comandante of the San Blas naval establishment, and while there, in 1791, made the draft of the Carta General of Spanish discoveries and explorations on the Californian and northwestern Pacific coast up to that year, which carta is the basis and the principal part of the map accompanying this volume. In 1792, De la Bodega was ordered to Nootka to take command of the Spanish forces, and to treat with Vancouver in the Nootka convention. He spent the winter of that year in California, and at Monterey royally entertained Vancouver upon his visit there. De la Bodega was born in Lima in 1744, and died at San Blas in March, 1794.

## PAGE 14   474/vi

S. Carlos = the paquebote San Carlos, or El Toisón de Oro
( = the Golden Fleece).

The San Carlos is famous in the history of California as the first vessel known
to have passed through La Bocana de la Ensenada de los Farallones (so called by
Don Pedro Fages in 1772), the present Golden Gate.   The San Carlos, with the
San Antonio or El Príncipe, was built at San Blas in 1768, as a supply-ship to be
used in connection with the new Franciscan establishments in Nueva California.
She was a boat "of eleven sails," of not more than two hundred tons burden, and
had been hastily and imperfectly constructed.   Her first voyage was to Guaymas, in Sonora, in
March, 1768, carrying troops thereto for the suppression of Indian uprisings.   Returning to San
Blas, she was partially laden with supplies for the proposed new establishments at San Diego and
Monterey, and her consort was the San Antonio.   These two vessels constituted the sea division
of "la santa expedición" of Gálvez for the spiritual conquest of Nueva California.   The San
Carlos was dispatched under the command of Vicente Vila, with orders to touch at La Paz, in
Antigua California, to take on board the members of the expedition who were to go by sea, and
to complete her cargo of supplies.   Arriving at La Paz on December 15th in a damaged condition after a stormy passage, necessary repairs compelled her to remain there until January 10,
1769, when she sailed for San Diego, arriving there on April 29th, with scurvy on board, some
of the crew having died therefrom, and the passage being stormy with heavy seas.   Conditions
were so bad that the continuation of the voyage to Monterey was abandoned.   After lying in
San Diego fifteen months, the San Carlos left there in August, 1770, for San Blas.   In February,
1771, the San Carlos left San Blas with missionaries for Antigua California, but was driven by
fierce northwesters nearly to Panamá, but reached Loreto on August 23d.   The San Carlos was
again at San Diego in August, 1772, under Don Miguel del Pino, together with the San Antonio
under Pérez, with supplies for the northern establishments, but, the winds being adverse, the San
Carlos discharged all her cargo at San Diego, although Pérez, on the pressing solicitation of the
Padre Presidente Serra, proceeded to Monterey.   The San Carlos, with Serra as a passenger on
his way to visit the Viceroy Bucareli at Mexico, sailed for San Blas on October 20th, and arrived
there on November 4th.   In the late spring of 1773, the San Carlos, under Don Juan Pérez, left
San Blas for San Diego and Monterey, with supplies, but in a storm off Cabo de San Lucas the
rudder was lost and a leak sprung.   The vessel was run up the gulf to Loreto, and the cargo
discharged.   Return was made to San Blas.   This caused a bitter famine at Monterey, which
was not relieved until the arrival of the Santiago, under Pérez, on May 9, 1774, on the first Bucareli expedition north of California.   On March 16, 1775, the San Carlos sailed from San Blas with
the second Bucareli expedition.   The fleet leaving San Blas at this time was composed of — 1. The
Santiago or Nueva Galicia, and La Sonora or La Felicidad; and 2. The San Carlos or El Toisón
de Oro.   The Santiago and the Sonora were on a voyage of discovery, as stated in the Journal,
but it is not evident therefrom that the San Carlos was in any way connected with the other
vessels.   The San Carlos, with supplies for Monterey, had run aground in the port of San Blas
on February 1st, and, following this, it was decided that supplies should also be carried for Anza's
Sonora colonists (pobladores) at San Francisco, and for the proposed new Franciscan establishments there, as well as to make a reconnoissance of that port, in order to determine whether the
bocana seen by Fages in 1772 was navigable, and also to seek for the strait supposed to connect
the old harbor of San Francisco with the new.   Don Bruno Heceta, the comandante of the expedition, had orders to assist in this reconnoissance, as had also Don Juan Bautista de Anza.   The
facts are set out farther along in this note.   Don Miguel Manrique, the comandante of the

San Carlos, having been declared insane, was sent back to San Blas, and Don Juan Manuel Ayala, the comandante of the Sonora, was ordered to the command of the San Carlos. On the return of the launch on March 21st, Ayala set sail. Don José Cañizares was the primero piloto and Don Juan Bautista Aguirre the segundo piloto of the San Carlos, and Padre Vicente de Santa María was chaplain. The passage to Monterey was stormy, slow, and not without incident. Ayala was seriously wounded in one foot by the accidental discharge of a pistol, and the launch caught fire while being calked with hot pitch. Punta de Pinos was sighted on June 25th, and the San Carlos, in the evening, anchored in the port of Monterey, "after one hundred and one days of navigation," and on the 26th the launch carried the mail ashore. This mail was of much importance. There was a letter from the Viceroy Bucareli to the Padre Presidente Serra at the Misión San Carlos, informing him that a land expedition was to leave Sonora, under the command of Don Juan Bautista de Anza, for Monterey, with troops and their families, and cattle and supplies, for the proposed new Franciscan establishments at the port of San Francisco. Don Fernando Xavier de Rivera y Moncada, the comandante militar at Monterey, was also informed of this expedition, and notified that the same was to be under his command upon the arrival of Anza, who was to assist Ayala, in the San Carlos, in the survey of the new port of San Francisco, and also to fix the sites for the proposed establishments. Bucareli did not fail in laying stress upon the necessity of co-operation, which failed in realization. (See notes post, to page 58, on San Francisco, to page 59, on Rivera, et passim.) The tempestuous weather encountered after leaving San Blas had damaged the San Carlos, entailing repairs at Monterey. A cayuco, or dug-out, was made on the Rio del Carmelo from the trunk of a redwood, to assist in the work of exploration. All needed preparations made, the San Carlos, on July 27th, left Monterey for the new port of San Francisco, and arrived off the entrance on August 5th. The launch, with the primero piloto Cañizares in command, and a crew of ten men, was sent in at eight in the morning to search for an anchorage. Night coming on, and the launch not returning, the San Carlos, with full sails, and not making more than a mile and a half an hour owing to the swiftness of the current, sought an anchorage, and, carefully sounding all the way, passed through the narrow strait now known as the Golden Gate, and, at half-past ten that night, — Saturday, August 5, 1775, — anchored without difficulty within the present Fort Point, named by them Punta de San José, — the first vessel to pass through the strait. The place of anchorage is supposed to have been east of the punta, off the present Presidio, and a little north of the anchorage indicated on the chart of Cañizares. (See this chart, inset in large map accompanying this volume.) At six o'clock the next morning the launch came to the San Carlos, having been prevented by whirlpools and eddies from returning on the day before. The place of anchorage was then changed to one on the north side of the bay, named by them Ensenada del Carmelita (= Bay of the Carmelite), a rock therein resembling a friar of that order. The present name is Richardson's Bay. The Indians everywhere manifested a friendly disposition. Cañizares and Padre Vicente de Santa María, with an armed crew, went ashore in the launch, taking beads and trinkets with them as presents, and the Indians entertained them with pinole and tamales. A better anchorage was found at a near-by island, which they named La Isla de Nuestra Señora de los Ángeles. The name still clings to this island, but in a clipped and mutilated form, — Angel Island. The place of anchorage was in the present Hospital Cove, probably. The work of exploration was then begun, principal among the purposes of which was to discover what connection existed between the new port of San Francisco and the old port, that is, the Puerto de San Francisco of Cermeño or Drakes Bay. Cañizares, the primero piloto, examined the extension of the bay to the northward, and Aguirre, the segundo piloto, was sent southward to seek the expected Rivera overland expedition, which was, among other things, to assist in the survey of the bay. Aguirre, acting under instructions, examined the southern part of the bay, and bestowed names upon several places, but the overland expedition did not arrive. Don Bruno Heceta, on his return from the north in the Santiago, had made an attempt to enter the harbor, but dense fogs prevented an entrance. Later, however, he headed a party to assist in this survey, but, arriving after the San Carlos had left the harbor, he is entitled merely to the doubtful honor of rendering socorro de España (= assistance that comes too late). (See ante, page 84, note on Heceta; see also post, note to page 58, on San Francisco.) The survey completed, and no land expedition having arrived, Padre Santa María, the chaplain, and a party climbed the hill named by them Punta del Ángel de la Guarda (the present Point Lobos), and, at the foot of the cross erected there by Rivera in 1774, deposited two letters to inform the land expedition, should it arrive later, of the then existing facts. The San Carlos was not to leave the harbor without a mishap. On September 7th, after weighing anchor to return to Monterey, the wind failed, and a strong current carried her upon a submerged rock near Punta Caballo, and her rudder was damaged. She put into what is now known as Horseshoe Bay for repairs, and while here the entrance to the port was more fully examined. Anchor was weighed on September 18th. The cayuco was lost on the preceding day. Monterey was reached the next day, and here Ayala found the Santiago, which had arrived from the north on August 29th. The Sonora arrived on October 7th. Further repairs on the San Carlos being necessary, Ayala could not leave for San Blas until October 13th. He arrived there on November 6th, and on the 9th sent his report to the Viceroy Bucareli, and his connection with the second Bucareli expedition was ended. On March 10, 1776, the San Carlos again sailed from San Blas, under the command of Fernando Quirós, and with José Cañizares as primero piloto and Cristóbal Revilla as segundo piloto, and Padres Vicente de Santa María and José Nocedal as chaplains. She arrived at Monterey on June 3d. Besides supplies for the establishments there, she also carried supplies for the proposed new establishments at San Francisco, and had orders from the Viceroy Bucareli to take on board the property of the colonists (= pobladores) Anza had recruited in Sonora. Some of the soldiers for the new Presidio were also carried when she sailed. The voyage from San Blas had been slow, but after leaving Monterey the San Carlos was at the mercy of unfavorable winds, which drove her south to San Diego and then far north of San Francisco. Monterey was left on June 5th, and San Francisco reached on August 18th, when the San Carlos passed through the Golden Gate for the second time. The land expedition, consisting of Anza's pobladores and padres for the founding of the new Presidio and Misión, had been anxiously awaiting the coming of the San Carlos, and her officers, crew, and chaplains assisted in the ceremonies attendant upon the founding. The comandante Quirós and José Joaquín Moraga, Anza's lieutenant, who commanded the land expedition from Monterey, made a reconnoissance to discover another entrance from the sea, of course with no result. On October 21st the San Carlos sailed for San Blas. In May, 1778, she was again at San Diego from the home port. In the autumn of 1779 the San Carlos, again under Ayala, was dispatched to the Philippines, with treasure to cover the expense of fortifications against the English. No further record of her is found. Her place as a supply-ship on the Californian coast was taken by another San Carlos, otherwise called El Filipino, and this vessel was lost in the Bay of San Francisco on March 23, 1797.

## Lieutenant D. Miguel Maurrique = Don Miguel Manrique, teniente de navío.

The rank of Manrique was higher than that of Ayala and De la Bodega, who were tenientes de fragata. An idea of rank in the Spanish royal navy (= real armada) may be gathered from the naval record of Ayala, page 89, ante. Manrique's patronymic is misspelled also on page 15, but the above correction is deemed sufficient.

## Monterey, and the Misión San Carlos Borromeo.

The "establishment at Monterey" referred to on page 14 is Misión San Carlos Borromeo de Monterey, founded on June 3, 1770, the second of the Franciscan establishments in Nueva California. The founders of the Misión were the Padres Junípero Serra and Juan Crespi. Don Gaspar de Portolá and Don Juan Pérez, the latter then comandante of the paquebote San Antonio, with military and naval supports, were present at the foundation ceremonies, after which Portolá took formal possession of the country in the name of Don Carlos III. In December, 1771, Misión San Carlos was moved to the banks of the Rio del Carmelo; hence the mutilated and now familiar name, "Carmel Mission." Here the Padre Presidente Serra made his headquarters, and here he died, August 28, 1784, and was buried in the Misión church. Barrington, of course, is in error when he, in the note on page 14, speaks of this establishment as a "mission of Jesuits"; the Jesuits had no missions in Nueva California. Monterey, under Spanish rule, was always considered the capital of Nueva California, military and civil. The Bay of Monterey is probably the Bahía de los Pinos of Juan Rodríguez Cabrillo, the discoverer of Nueva California in 1542. By some writers it is identified as the San Pedro of Sebastián Rodríguez Cermeño (1595). Don Sebastián Vizcaíno, in December 1602, named it Puerto de Monterey, in honor of the Viceroy, the Conde de Monterey. (See note to page 21, post, on Aguilar.) Don Gaspar de Portolá, in his land expedition of 1769, failed to identify the port, and, passing it and proceeding northward, the new port of San Francisco was accidentally discovered. Don Juan Bautista de Anza arrived here in April, 1774, on his memorable journey which established an overland route from Sonora to the sea, and found the inhabitants on the verge of starvation. He was here again in March, 1776, on his way to San Francisco, with troops and their families and colonists for the proposed establishments there. (See note post, to page 58, on San Francisco.)

## PAGE 15   7/475

On the 13th = On the 19th.

## PAGE 17   9/477

Hernando Triabba = Hernando de Grijalva.

Grijalva was sent by the great Cortés, together with Diego Bezerra de Mendoza, on a voyage of discovery in the year 1533,—Bezerra, in command of the expedition, in La Concepción, with Fortuño Ximénez, a Vizcaíno, as piloto, and Grijalva in command of el San Lázaro, with Martín de Acosta as piloto. The vessels sailed from Tehuantepec on the 0th of October, separated the second night out,—by design, it is said, Bezerra being haughty in disposition. Grijalva discovered the group of islands now called the Revillagigedos, landing on the island of Socorro on St. Thomas's Day (December 20th), and naming it Santo Tomás. It is worthy of note here that Bezerra, after the separation from Grijalva, was murdered while asleep, upon the mutiny of the crew, by his piloto Ximénez, who thereupon took command of La Concepción. Returning, he accidentally discovered Baja California, at Santa Cruz Bay, in 1534, and was thus that the California of fact —not the fabular or mythical California—became known. The natives, however, killed Ximénez. Grijalva, in 1535, was the commander of a vessel in a fleet sailing on an another voyage of discovery, under the personal command of Cortés.

### Guantepec = Tehuantepec.

### Hernan Cortes.

Both the prænomen and the patronymic of Cortés are variously spelled; thus, Hernán, Hernando; Cortés, Cortez. He was born at Medellín, near Badajoz, Estremadura, in 1485; died near Seville, December 2, 1547. His rise, career, and end were truly Moorish; elevated from nothing, he conquered kingdoms, trampled on foreign kings, and was rewarded by his own with ingratitude. He was a fine specimen of a Spanish guerrillero. His types were Sertorious, Al-Mansur, the Cid. His system was a combination of the Moorish algihad or crusade and the Spanish algara or foray. His were the besetting sins of both Moor and Spaniard,—avarice, cruelty, bloodshed, bigotry, and bad faith, gilded by a chivalrous, bold, lofty, adventurous daring and talent. Indignant at the ingratitude of Charles V. (Don Carlos I of Spain), he returned to Nueva España and sought to extend his fame by maritime discovery, particularly in the opening of a passage from the Atlantic to the Pacific, and it was in one of the expeditions fitted out at his expense that the coast of the Californias was discovered, and his were the ships that first sailed these northwestern seas.

## Sotovento = Sotavento.

## Page 18  478/10

## Errors, typographical or otherwise.

In Barrington's table of "Corrections of the more Material Errors,"'at the end of his work, he notes one in this page; namely, that the word "the," ending the sixth line from the foot of the page, should be "their" (their business). This error, it will be perceived, stands unchanged in this edition. Compared with some errors appearing in the Journal, this one is trifling. Such errors as "blowng," in the second line of page 18, are unchanged and unnoted, although misspelling etc. of Spanish terms are generally corrected in these Notes, for obvious reasons.

## Page 19  11/479

## Chuvascos (pl.) = Chubasco or chubazo (sing.).

A Spanish nautical term. Its use is not confined to the Mexican seas.

## Page 20  480/12

## Martín de Aguilar.

Aguilar was the comandante of Los Tres Reyes, with Antonio Flórez as piloto, in Sebastián Vizcaíno's expedition to the coast of Nueva California in 1602–03. This expedition, in which three vessels were engaged, sailed from Acapulco on May 5, 1602. They were at San Diego on November 10th, and this place was so named in honor of their flagship, in disregard of the name of San Miguel given it by Cabrillo in 1542. On December 16th they were at Monterey, which was so named in honor of the Viceroy, the Conde de Monterey (Gaspar de Zúñiga y Azevedo), and the Rio del Carmelo was also named, in honor of the Carmelite chaplain accompanying them. Here the Santo Tomás was sent back to Acapulco with the scurvy-stricken, and the expedition sailed northward on January 3, 1603. Passing the Farallones (named Frailes on Vizcaíno's map), the present Drakes Bay was named Puerto de los Reyes or Puerto de Don Gaspar. This puerto was named San Francisco in 1595 by Cermeño, and here his galleon, the San Agustín, was wrecked. Just north of Punta de los Reyes, Vizcaíno's vessels were separated in a storm on January 7th, and he turned back to search for the wreck of the San Agustín. He afterwards headed north. Both vessels reached the latitude of Cabo Blanco. The voyage throughout was one of hardship and suffering. The San Diego, under Vizcaíno, reached Acapulco in March. Aguilar and his piloto Flórez died on the voyage home. Estévan López, listed as a corporal, acted as piloto of Los Tres Reyes, and arrived at Acapulco in February, with only three men. Sir Daines, in note *e* to page 20, is incorrect in giving the year of this voyage as 1601, and also in speaking of the supposed discovery of a river as having been made ''by the pilot Lopes.'' Flórez was the piloto, and it was by him that the supposed discovery was made, and Venegas is miscited. The identity of the river is not established.

## PAGE 21   13/481

El remorque = El remolque (= the towing-rope).

## PAGE 22   482/14

We saw likewise the frigate at the bottom of the port.

The first sentence of the last paragraph of this page is rendered obscure either by mistranslation or mispunctuation. The meaning possibly is, that they found sufficient depth of water in which to anchor, at a bow's-shot from the land which they, as well as the frigate, saw at the bottom of the port. The Sonora, it will be noted, preceded the frigate.

## PAGE 23   15/483

Cape Fortuna = the Cabo de Fortunas of the Spaniards (= the cape of storms).

The name was applied by Bartolomé Ferrelo, the Levantine piloto of Cabrillo, in the expedition of 1542–43, and the cape is identified by some writers with Cape Mendocino.

Cape Mendocino = the Cabo de Mendozino of the Spaniards.

By whom and when the name of this cape was first applied is not definitely known; but it was so named in honor of Antonio de Mendoza, the first viceroy of México.

## PAGE 24   484/16

We named the port [Puerto de la Santísima Trinidad].

It will be noted that this port was discovered on the 9th of June, and that possession was not taken, nor a landing made, until the 11th. Sir Daines, in note *o*, page 24, recognizes the ''use to geographers in this custom of the Spaniards naming places from the saint's day in which they take possession, or make the discovery.'' Little, if any, attention is paid to the distinction here noted, and the 11th of June is usually given as the date of the discovery of this port, and this, too, by authors regarded as authoritative. (See note to page 30, post, as to this port.)

### St. George's Sound = Nootka Sound.

This sound was discovered by Don Juan Pérez in the first Bucareli expedition in 1774, and named by him Puerto de San Lorenzo. Captain James Cook, in 1778, deeming himself its discoverer, named it St. George's Sound, but afterwards decided to retain the name used by the natives,— Nootka.

## PAGE 25    17/485

Peinado en castanna = Peinado en castaña.

Azarcón = of an orange-color.    Azul = blue.

## PAGE 26    486/18

Beard = Barba.    Chin = Barba.    (Homonymy.)

Colgadas par [por] las mesillas.

Lip-pieces or lip-ornaments.

These are described in the writings of early explorers and travelers.  Sir Daines, in note *a*, unnecessarily expresses a doubt of the intelligibility of his translated description.

## PAGE 27    19/487

Á la oración = at sunset.

Las oraciones (pl.) = sunsetting, when the angel's salutation to the Virgin is repeated by the people.   Oración = a prayer, a declamation, an oration, etc.

## PAGE 30    490/22

Chart the 6th.

The nine charts referred to on this page are not known to be in existence, and regret is often expressed at their evident loss.  The three inset charts in the upper right-hand corner of the large map accompanying this book are presumed to have been redrawn from the originals mentioned on page 30, and sent to Madrid by De la Bodega with his Carta General. It would be interesting to know if De la Bodega had the chart of Trinidad at that time.  It must be noted that the Ayala chart is an addition to the original Carta General, as are also the ornamental contemporary copperplate designs, and the English title of the map.

## PAGE 32    492/24

Pigeon = Pichón.

The word used by the journalist was probably "tórtola" (= turtle-dove), and not "pichón."  The river is the Rio de las Tórtolas of the old maps, and is that now known at Little Trinidad River.

Trinity Harbour = Puerto de la Santísima Trinidad.

See note on Heceta, ante, page 85.

## PAGE 33    25/493

John de Fuca = Juan de Fuca.

A Greek whose name was Apostolos Valerianos.  His voyage is mythical.

## PAGE 37   29/497

### On the 1st [14th] of July.

The 14th is the correct day of the month, as the context will show.

### Pedro Santa Ana, contramaestre (= boatswain) of the Sonora.

This is the only instance in the Journal where the personal name of a member of the crew is set out, and it is to be regretted that the landing-party died unavenged. The place where the massacre occurred was named Punta y Ensenada de los Mártires (= the point and the bay of the martyrs), and the island to the north thereof, Isla de los Dolores (= the island of grief). (See the large map; and for the crew of the Sonora, see ante, note to page 13.)

## PAGE 41   33/501

### [On] the 4th, . . . 17 [170] leagues W. of the continent.

### Lady of Bethlem [Bethlehem] = Nuestra Señora de Belén.

## PAGE 42   502/34

### St. Jacinthus = San Jacinto.

This mountain is not indicated on the large map, but it is identified with Mount Edgecumbe (so named by Captain Cook), on Kruzof Island.

### Cape del Enganno = Cabo del Engaño.

The Spanish name of this cape is translated into English as "False Cape" and "Cape Deceit," etc., by some writers. As the Spanish "engaño" means, also, mistake, misunderstanding, misconception, attempts to render an English equivalent thereof are not justified, in the absence of a reason for the bestowal of the name.

### The chart of Don Juan Pérez.

Sir Daines is in error when, in note *e*, he supposes the chart was that of Pérez. De la Bodega, in a report of the occurrences of this day, speaks only of the charts of Bellin. Besides, Pérez, in 1774, had reached only 55° N., and his observations were not good, owing to fogs and bad weather.

## PAGE 44   504/36

### De los Remedios = Puerto de Nuestra Señora de los Remedios.

This port is the Bay of Islands of Captain Cook. (See the large map accompanying this volume, for the chart of this port, as made by De la Bodega and Maurelle.)

## PAGE 46   506/38

### These Indians eradicate their beard.

Sir Daines evidently knew nothing of the ingenuity exercised in this practice.

## PAGE 48   508/40

### Beering = Vitus Bering (or Behring).   (1680–1741.)

Bering was a Danish navigator in the Russian service.   He perished from cold
and exhaustion upon his ship being wrecked on the coast of the island which now bears his name.

### Tschirikow = Alexeï Ilich Chirikof.

This Russian navigator discovered Alaska in 1741.   The Aleutian island Chirikof perpetuates his name.   He died in 1747.

### Straits of Admiral Fonte, and the Archipelago of S. Lazarus.

There is nothing substantial about either the supposed person or places.

## PAGE 49   41/509

### This *arm* . . . is delineated in one of our charts.

The "arm" is marked "Puerto de Bucarely" on the large map, and "Pto.
Bucarely" on the small map, accompanying this volume.   The chart referred to is undoubtedly
that sent by De la Bodega to Madrid with his Carta General, and redrawn for insertion therein.
(See the large map;  and see also note to page 30, on page 97, ante.)

### Corral = A yard inclosed with pickets or stakes;  a pen.

## PAGE 50   510/42

### Sailed on the 29th.

The 26th was probably the day of sailing.

## PAGE 51   43/511

### Errors or inconsistencies.

There are some inconsistencies both in this page and in that following.   Thus
in the first paragraph of this page, it is said that "the health of our crews was re-
established";  in the third paragraph, that "the two ships divided some cloaths";  and in note *z*,
that "the two ships were now to sail N.";  while in the first paragraph of page 52 it is said that
scurvy was caught "from the seamen of the frigate, with whom we had occasional communication."   These errors may be the result of mistranslation, and no attempt will here be made to
account for them.   The Santiago had not been seen since the end of July, and was near or in
the port of Monterey at the times mentioned in the text.   Lapses such as these, and worse, are
often found by proof-readers in the MS. of good writers.

## PAGE 55   47/515

### Fule = Tule.

This is the Spanish-American name of a bulrush or clubrush.   There are two
varieties of tule, — *Scirpus lacustris and S. occidentalis*.   Sir Daines, of course, in note *g*, on this
page, is wide of the mark.   The rude tule rafts or canoes were termed *balsas*.

## PAGE 56   516/48

### This port, which we named de *la Bodega* = Puerto de la Bodega.

This name survives, but, like many other Spanish place-names, only in a clipped form,— Bodega. The Spaniards were given to this reprehensible practice of mutilating names, both of persons and places, and their English-speaking successors, who have "entered into the fruits of their labors," continued the practice. It is, of course, at this late day, impossible to know who is responsible for "La Bodega," found in Forbes's History of California,— whether the native Hispano-Californians, or the American and English seamen trading on the coast. All were probably ignorant of the name of the discoverer of the port, and there is hardly a doubt that they associated the name "Bodega" with the storehouse built there by the Russians, who first came in 1809, and who remained there until 1840, a thorn in the side of both Spain and México. The Spanish word "bodega" means a warehouse, a storeroom, a cellar, a wine-vault, and the term is also applied to a bibulous individual. A chart of the port, made by De la Bodega y Quadra, is reproduced in his Carta General as in inset. (See the large map accompanying this volume.) Another chart of the bay, stated by Bancroft to be "the original Spanish map made at the discovery of the bay by Bodega y Cuadra in 1775," is printed on page 81 of the second volume of his History of California. These charts are not identical, and that of Bancroft is not a facsimile of the purported original. No place-names are given in the inset chart in the large map, but in the Bancroft chart the present Tomales Bay is marked "Mar ó Rio" (= sea or river), which is merely descriptive; the land lying to the east of this bay is marked "Campo Verde" (= green flat and open country), which is also descriptive; but only the northern part of Tomales Bay is charted, and the two puntas at its mouth are marked in consonance with the names as given by the journalist in pages 56 and 57; thus, Punta Arenas (= point of the sands), the present Sand Point; Pta. [Punta] del Cordon (= point of the cord), the present Tomales Point. Bodega Head is marked "Pta. de Munguia" (probably named in honor of Padre José Antonio Murguía). Bodega Rock, off the eastern end of this punta, is marked "Farallon del Padre Sierra" (Padre Benito Sierra). As but few soundings are given in the Bancroft chart, and these at the mouth of the bay only, those in the inset chart in the large map must have been taken from some of the later surveys. De la Bodega regarded Tomales Bay as the mouth of a large river (see page 54), and this, after the survey of the harbor of San Francisco by Ayala, gave rise to the supposition that it was connected in some way with that harbor. It is supposed that De la Bodega regarded Bodega and Tomales bays as one bay. Captain Beechey so regarded them. The name "Tomales," as applied to the bay, is said to be derived from the Tamal Indians (so called) of the San Rafael and Sonoma Franciscan missions, whose home was in the vicinity of the bay, and whose name for any bay, and particularly their own, was "tamal." When Vancouver was there in 1792 it was known as Juan Francisco, and in the Vizcaíno chart of 1603 it is laid down as a river and named the Rio Grande de San Sebastián.

### Note *i*. The latitude of this harbour coincides nearly with that discovered by Sir Francis Drake.

The three bays within a short distance of one another — Bodega, Drakes, and San Francisco — have each and all been identified as Drake's place of anchorage. Drakes Bay is the Puerto de San Francisco of Sebastián Rodríguez Cermeño, the comandante of the galleon San Agustin, which was wrecked there in 1595. It was visited by Sebastián Vizcaíno in 1603, and named Puerto de los Reyes, or Puerto de Don Gaspar. Here Drake overhauled his vessel, the Golden Hinde, in 1579. Besides its present name of Drakes Bay, it is sometimes referred to as the old port or harbor of San Francisco. It is the Jack's Harbor of the early American sailors.

## Sir Francis Drake.

Laden with immense booty obtained by despoiling Spanish towns on the coasts of Chile and Perú, and with treasure taken from richly laden royal Spanish galleon and Spanish merchantman, there rounded the Punta de los Reyes, from the north, on the seventeenth day of June, 1579, a vessel of some one hundred tons burden, and anchored in the bay lying thereunder. This vessel was the Golden Hinde, and her commander was Francis Drake. He had been seeking a northeast passage to the Atlantic, and had reached 48° N., but his crew dreaded the severe cold, and besides, the Golden Hinde was in need of repairs. While his men were repairing the ship, Drake established friendly relations with the Indians, although he had taken the precaution to build a bulwark of stone to protect his crew. He took possession of the country in the name of Queen Elizabeth, and named it New Albion, the white cliffs along the coast reminding him of those of England. To the harbor itself it does not appear that Drake applied any name, but the Farallones were named the Islands of Saint James. No diary or log of the Golden Hinde is known to be in existence, if, indeed, any was kept; hence the narratives of the voyage vary in many particulars. Drake left the harbor which now bears his name on July 23, 1579, having spent five weeks therein, and sailed direct to the North Farallon, and thence to the South Farallon. He and his crew landed on the latter on the 24th,—the first Europeans, and possibly the first of the human race, to set foot there,—which ''have thereon plentifull and great stores of seales and birds,'' which ''are good meat, and are an acceptable food for us at present, and a good supply of our provision for the future.'' They sailed from the South Farallon on the 25th, and, following the route taken by Magellan, steered across the Pacific for the Moluccas, thence to Java, thence to the Cape of Good Hope, and thence homeward, arriving at Plymouth on Sunday, September 26, 1579. Drake was the eldest of twelve sons of a poor and obscure Puritan yeoman, and he grew up among sailors, his father, who had secured an appointment to read prayers to seamen in the royal navy, by reason of his poverty was compelled to apprentice him to the master of a bark. Drake subsequently became the owner of the bark, which he afterwards sold, and embarked himself and his fortunes in Sir John Hawkins's unfortunate expedition to the Spanish Main. Losing all his money, a chaplain comforted him with the assurance that, having been treacherously treated by the Spaniards, the law of retaliation was applicable against the king of Spain. He died on December 27, 1595, upon the breaking out of a fatal disease among the men of the fleet sent out that year to the West Indies against the Spaniards. Drake undoubtedly, more than any other man, was the founder of England's naval greatness, but, unless judged by the standards of his time, he must appear, in many of his exploits, in no other light than that of a skillful and daring buccaneer.

## PAGE 57   49/517

## Cape, which appeared to the S. = Punta de los Reyes.

This cape or point is the northern limit of the Ensenada de los Farallones of the Spaniards, the Gulf of the Farallones of the United States government charts, and the point itself is the present Point Reyes. The Spanish name was given by Don Sebastián Vizcaíno in 1603, with an alias, Punta de Don Gaspar. ''Los Reyes'' were the Magi (Sp., Magos = kings, wise men),—the New Testament ''wise men from the east '' (Sp., Magos vinierón del oriente). There are at least three traditions as to who the Magi were, and their names. As, according to one tradition, Gaspar was the name of one, and as this name was the prænomen of the viceroy of Nueva España (Don Gaspar de Zúñiga y Azevedo), doubt is expressed as to whom Vizcaíno meant to honor in applying the alias. The same names were given to the harbor (=puerto) lying under the point (= punta).  Vizcaíno's ships had left Monterey on January 3, 1603, in search of the Cabo de Mendozino, and were tempest-tossed on their way northward, but the tempest ceased on January 6th, Twelfth-Day (El Dia de la Adoración de los Reyes), when they were carried beyond the Puerto de los Reyes.  The next day Vizcaíno returned to the puerto to search for the wreck of the galleon San Agustín, which, in 1595, under Sebastián Rodríguez Cermeño, was driven behind the punta and wrecked, and it is supposed that it was at this time that the name of Puerto de San Francisco was applied to the present Drakes Bay.  (See ante, page 95, note on Martin Aguilar.)  Both the punta and the puerto were probably sighted by the Cabrillo expedition of 1542, and possibly also by Cabrillo's piloto mayor Ferrelo the next year, and Drake overhauled the Golden Hinde in the puerto in the summer of 1579, but there is no record found that any of these gave a name to either puerto or punta.

## We sailed near those small islands [Farallones].

The Spanish word "farallón" (pron., sing. *far-al-yone'*, pl. *far-al-yo'-nays*) means, in English, a small pointed island in the sea, or a large isolated rock above the water.  The term is purely nautical.  Those farallones lying off the coast of the Gulf of the Farallones, that is, from Point Reyes on the north to Point San Pedro on the south, are not now known by any of their old Spanish names, being simply called the Farallones or the Farallon Islands, and these are their names as set out in maps and dictionaries, although the name "Farallon Islands" is an improper combination; as well might one say "stone rocks."  The name, however, is fixed.  The group is disposed in a general west-northwest and east-southeast direction for seven nautical miles.  The South Farallon is the principal one, being the largest and highest.  It lies twenty-three nautical miles off the Golden Gate.  It is three quarters of a mile long in its longest direction, and three fifths of a mile wide at its greatest breadth, not including half a dozen high rocky islets under its shores.  The principal peak at the south has an elevation of 340 feet.  The whole island is wild, barren, and desolate; it is the outcrop of an immense dike of granite, but the condition of the superficial parts is such that they can be separated into small fragments by pick or crowbar.  North-northwest from this peak is Sugarloaf Rock, a rounded, almost vertical rocky islet, nearly two hundred feet above the sea.  From the extreme northwest point of the South Farallon the Middle Farallon bears northwest 1¾ miles.  It is a single black rock, between 50 and 60 yards in diameter, 22 feet above water, and lies, northwest by west, 2¼ miles from the South Farallon.  The North Farallon is composed of a group of four islets and one rock.  The four large ones have a roughly pyramidal appearance.  All are comprised within a space four fifths of a mile west-northwest and east-southeast by one fifth of a mile in breadth.  They are wild, rocky, precipitous, and almost inaccessible.  The Farallones were probably seen for the first time by Europeans by the Cabrillo and Ferrelo expedition in 1542.  Francis Drake, in 1579, named them the Islands of Saint James, and landed on the South Farallon on his way home.  (See note ante, page 101.)  Don Sebastián Vizcaíno, in January, 1603, passed the Farallones, and in the chart made by his cosmographer, Gerónimo Martín Palacios, the North Farallon group is marked "Frailes" (sing., fraile = friar or brother); hence the Spanish name, Farallones de los Frailes, applied to the whole group, and this is the name used by Ringgold in his chart of 1850.  The South Farallon in the Vizcaíno chart is called the Isleo Hendido (isleo = an island composed of rocks, without any visible means of access; hendido == crannied), this name being descriptive.  Don Miguel Costansó, the engineer of the Portolá expedition of 1769, when the present Bay of San Francisco was discovered, speaks of them as the Farallones del Puerto de San Francisco.  It is not definitely known when or by whom the Spanish name "Farallones de San Francisco" was first given.  La Ensenada de los Farallones is the present Gulf of the Farallones, and La Bocana de la Ensenada de los Farallones is the Golden Gate.

## PAGE 58   518/50

# Harbour of St. Francis.

The port here referred to by the journalist is the present harbor of San Francisco; but on page 54 he confuses it with the harbor mentioned by Venegas in his History of California, that is, the Puerto de San Francisco of Cermeño, the present Drakes Bay, the Jack's Harbor of the American sailor. Some of the older Spanish navigators regarded the Ensenada de los Farallones —the Gulf of the Farallones of the United States government charts—as the Puerto de San Francisco. The boundaries of this gulf or ensenada were, the Farallones de San Francisco on the west, and on the east, from Punta de los Reyes on the north to Punta San Pedro on the south. But consideration of the old harbor of San Francisco may be dismissed here. Wonder is often expressed that so extensive a body of water as the present Bay of San Francisco should escape observation until its accidental discovery by a soldier in the Portolá expedition of 1769, by land, and not by sea. The fogs, the narrowness of the entrance, the fact that the Spanish maritime explorers did not go very far inland, were sufficient to keep the bay a secret. Portolá, on his march from San Diego to Monterey to found at the latter port a royal presidio and a Franciscan misión, having passed the port without recognizing it, continued on his march northward, and at length came within sight of Punta de los Reyes, which the charts enabled the party to identify at once. José Francisco Ortega, a sargento of the soldados de cuera, was ordered to explore the coast to the punta, and he was allowed three days for this purpose and to report. This was on November 1, 1769, and the place from which he started was Punta San Pedro, named by this expedition La Punta de las Almejas del Ángel de la Guarda. Of course Ortega could not reach Punta de los Reyes overland, but he is regarded by some of the foremost authorities as the discoverer of the Bay of San Francisco, and also of the Golden Gate. He returned to camp on the third day and reported, but he was not the first to report to Portolá the existence of the bay. A number of soldiers had received permission to go deer-hunting on November 2d, and on their return the same day reported that they had seen the bay. Following the necessarily short survey of the bay by Ortega in 1769, Don Pedro Fages, teniente de Voluntarios de Cataluña, comandante militar of Nueva California after the departure of Portolá in 1770, left Monterey on November 21, 1770, on a reconnoitering expedition. He went as far as San Leandro Creek, on the Alameda Creek, and his men as far as the Strait of Carquínez. Again, on the 20th of March, 1772, Fages, now termed a capitán, left Monterey, with Padre Juan Crespi, on an expedition to the port of San Francisco to select a site for the proposed new misión of San Francisco, and on the 27th, from what is now Berkeley, saw the Golden Gate, which they named La Bocana de la Ensenada de los Farallones,—the first name applied by Europeans to the strait now known as the Golden Gate. Being on the east side of the bay, and having no boats, their efforts to reach the Puerto de los Reyes overland, after a long journey, were futile. To the waters embracing the present San Joaquín River, Carquínez Strait, and Suisún Bay they applied the name of Rio de Nuestro Padre San Francisco. Don Fernando Xavier Rivera y Moncada, who succeeded Fages in May, 1774, as comandante militar of Nueva California, left Monterey, in November of that year, on an expedition similar in purpose to those of Fages in 1770 and 1772. He was accompanied by the Padre Francisco Palou as chaplain and diarist. On Sunday, December 4th, they, with four soldiers, climbed the Punta de los Lobos, from which they saw the Golden Gate, and on the summit of the punta they raised a cross, found by the Heceta and Ayala parties of 1775. (See note ante, page 45, and see also infra.) The weather being unpropitious, the party returned to Monterey. The next expedition to the harbor of San Francisco was that of Ayala, in the San Carlos, in 1775. This, unlike those of Fages and Rivera, was not an independent expedition. It was an integral part of the second expedition sent north from San Blas by the great Viceroy Bucareli. Don Juan Bautista de Anza was to bring overland, from Sonora to Monterey, troops and their families for the founding of the new establishments at the harbor of San Francisco. At Monterey these were to be turned over to the command of Rivera, the comandante militar, and Anza was to assist Ayala in the survey of the bay. Don Bruno Heceta and De la Bodega, in the Santiago and Sonoro, on their return from the north, were also to assist in the survey. They had taken possession of territory in the north as recorded in the Journal, and ports had been charted, with the object of anticipating threatened aggressions by the Russians and English, and, at the same time, of protecting the coasts of the Californias. But Heceta could not enter the harbor on his return, owing to dense fogs; De la Bodega could not, having lost his boat, as stated in the Journal; and Anza did not leave Sonora in time to be of any assistance to Ayala. Rivera having orders to assist in the foundation of the new establishments, he, after some delay, furnished nine soldiers as a guard to an overland expedition under the command of Heceta. A carpenter and three sailors went along, and a small canoe was carried on muleback. The Padre Presidente Serra also sent Padre Francisco Palou, who was accompanied by Padre Miguel de la Campa y Cos, one of the chaplains on the Santiago. But Ayala had left San Francisco harbor before they arrived there. Thus no presidio or misión was established at San Francisco in 1775. (As to this Heceta overland expedition, see further, note on Heceta, ante, page 84.) Ayala in the San Carlos passed through the Golden Gate at half-past ten o'clock on the night of Saturday, August 5, 1775, and anchored inside the harbor, probably somewhat north of the place indicated by the anchor east of the Punta de San José of the Ayala inset chart in the large map accompanying this volume. Her permanent place of anchorage while making the survey was, in all probability, in what is now known as Hospital Cove, Angel Island, indicated by the anchor west of the island marked *b* in the chart (Isla de los Ángeles). The survey completed, the San Carlos left the harbor for Monterey on September 14th, the first vessel in which a survey was made of the present harbor of San Francisco, and the first vessel that passed through the narrow strait now known as the Golden Gate. (See further, notes on Ayala and the San Carlos, ante, pages 89, 91.) In the table in the Ayala chart, called "Explicación" (= explanation or interpretation), are given the place-names as applied either by Ayala or by his pilotos Cañizares and Aguirre. Of these, only two survive, namely, Angel Island and Alcatraz Island. Both the original and the present names follow.

Bosques de Palo Colorados = Redwood groves or forests.

Isla de los Ángeles = Angel Island.

Yerba Buena Island, or Goat Island, although referred to in the report of the piloto Cañizares, evidently received no name at that time, and the letter *c*, as marked on that island in the chart, is misplaced, as that letter, according to the Explicación, was meant to indicate the Isla de Alcatraces, which lies west of Yerba Buena Island.

Isla de Alcatraces (sing., alcatraz = pelican) = Alcatraz Island.

Bahía de Nuestra Señora del Rosario la Marinera = The sheet of water between Point San Pedro and Point San Pablo on the north and Tiburón Peninsula and Point Richmond on the south.

Punta del Ángel de la Guarda = Point Lobos.

Bahía de Nuestra Señora de Guadalupe = San Pablo Bay. Cañizares, in his report, calls this bay Bahía Redondo (= round bay).

Punta de San José = Fort Point. This is the Punta del Cantil Blanco of the Anza expedition of 1776, and later marked "Punta del Cantil Blanco y Fuerte de San Joaquín" on Spanish maps.

Puerta de la Asumpta = Southampton Bay. So named by Cañizares because they were there on August 15th, the feast of the Assumption.

Ranchería del Socorro (socorro = help, succor). On the south side of Carquínez Strait. At this ranchería the Indians were generous in gifts of fish, pinole, etc., to Cañizares and his party.

Ensenada de los Llorones (= mourners) = Mission Bay. So named by Aguirre because he saw some Indians weeping there.

Estero Seco (= dry) = Islais Creek.

Punta de Concha (= shell; oyster) = Point Avisadero.

Punta de San Antonio = Point Richmond.

Punta de Santiago = Point Bonita.
Punta de San Carlos = Lime Point.
Ensenada del Carmelita = Richardson's Bay.
Ensenada del Santo Evangelio = The cove between Tiburón and Belvedere.
Punta de Langosta (= locust; oyster) = Point San Pedro.
Isla Plana (= level, fruitful ground) = Mare Island.
Junta de los Quatro Evangelistas = Suisún Bay.
Rio de San Juan Bautista = San Joaquín River.

Don Juan Bautista de Anza, who, according to the plans of Bucareli, was to assist Ayala in the survey of the new port of San Francisco, and also in the founding of a pueblo, and a presidio for the protection of the proposed Franciscan establishments, did not leave Tubac, Sonora, until October 3, 1775, more than a month after Ayala had completed his survey, but during the time Heceta was seeking Ayala at the new port. (See note ante, page 84.) He was accompanied by troops and their families, with colonists (pobladores), with live-stock and other property. Ayala had brought to Monterey, on the San Carlos, supplies for the new establishments. These were, according to the instructions of Bucareli, discharged at Monterey to await the arrival of Anza, when Rivera, the comandante militar, was to take command of the expedition. Rivera, in the mean time, had gone to San Diego to protect the Franciscans there after an Indian revolt, and was at the Misión San Gabriel when Anza arrived there on January 4, 1776. Here Rivera persuaded Anza to accompany him to San Diego with some of his soldiers, the main body of the expedition being left at San Gabriel under the Teniente José Joaquín Moraga. At San Diego, Anza doubted the good faith of Rivera, who was not in accord with the padres, and cared nothing about the proposed establishments at San Francisco. Anza, to whom the latter were his chief concern, left San Diego for San Gabriel, where supplies were short, and from thence, on February 21st, with the expedition, proceeded to Monterey, which was reached on March 10th, and here, afterwards, a letter was received at the Presidio, from Rivera at San Diego, ordering the pobladores of Anza to erect houses for themselves at Monterey and await the erection of the Presidio at San Francisco. Anza thereupon wrote to Rivera, expressing the feelings of the pobladores and the padres, and on March 23d he set out for San Francisco, with Moraga, Padre Pedro Font, the chaplain of the expedition, a corporal and ten soldiers, and a pack-train. On the 26th they reached Punta de los Lobos, and found a part of the cross erected there by Rivera in 1774. From there they passed on to the present Fort Point, named by them Punta del Cantil Blanco (= the point of the precipitous white cliff), and here a cross was raised to mark where the fort (= fuerte) should be built, — the point and fort later called by the Spaniards the Punta del Cantil y Fuerte de San Joaquín. They encamped at Mountain Lake (Laguna del Presidio), and the stream running therefrom (Lobos Creek) they named Arroyo del Puerto (= the stream of the port). The adjoining mesa (= tableland), between Mountain Lake and Fort Point, was designated by Anza as the site for the new town. The Fresh Pond or Washerwoman's Lagoon of the American pioneers of San Francisco (the Laguna Pequeña of the Spaniards) was passed on the survey, and Alta Loma (Telegraph Hill) was climbed to obtain a view of the bay. Their encampment at Mountain Lake was broken up, and the shore of the bay was afterwards followed. La Ensenada de los Llorones (Mission Bay) was visited. Mission Creek was reached at the point where it drained the laguna fed by Willows Creek, and this laguna was named by them La Laguna de Manantial (= the lake of the flowing water). A pretty rivulet — ojo de agua — was found, and named Arroyo de los Dolores. The surroundings providing much that was necessary for a new mission establishment, Anza determined that this spot should be the site thereof. This was on March 29, 1776. Anza, on this expedition, proceeded as far as the Rio de Nuestro Padre San Francisco (so named by Fages in his expedition of 1772). Anza was convinced that this was not a river, but a fresh-water lake, and named it Puerto Dulce (= sweetwater harbor). On the return to México, the Anza expedition reached Monterey on Easter Monday morning, April 8, 1776.

On the 17th of June, 1776, there set out from Monterey an overland expedition for the founding of the Misión and the Presidio of San Francisco, and also of a pueblo. The comandante of this expedition was Teniente José Joaquín Moraga, with Sargento Juan Pablo Grijalva and also two corporals. There were sixteen soldiers and ten colonists, or pobladores, with their families. Pack-mules with supplies, and also two hundred cattle, were under the charge of Indians. The Padres Francisco Palou and Pedro Benito Cambón, with neophytes, had their own Indian servants, with other Indians to care for the cattle and also the pack-mules with the supplies for the new Misión. The site for the Misión, as determined upon by Anza, was reached on the 27th of June, and on the next day "una enramada" (a hut covered with branches of trees) was erected and an altar set up, and on the 29th (fiesta de los grandes santos apóstoles San Pedro y San Pablo) the first mass was celebrated, by the Padre Francisco Palou, at La Misión de Nuestro Seráfico Padre San Francisco de Asís. On the 26th of July, Moraga, with his soldiers and the pobladores, moved to the Presidio site and erected brushwood huts. The first one built was a chapel, and here, on July 28th, Padre Palou said the first mass at this place. The San Carlos, with supplies for the new establishments, from San Blas, was at Monterey when Moraga left there, but did not reach San Francisco until August 18th. (See note on the voyages of the San Carlos, ante, pages 91–93.) The crew of the San Carlos assisted in the erection of permanent buildings for the new establishments, and by the middle of September these structures were finished, and the ceremony of taking possession of the country was performed at the Presidio on September 17, 1776,—dia de las llagas de nuestro seráfico padre San Francisco, patrón del puerto, del nuevo Presidio, y de la Misión. Padre Francisco Palou was assisted in the religious ceremonies by the Padres Benito Cambón, Tomás de la Peña y Sarabia, Vicente Santa María, and José Nocedal, the two last named being the chaplains of the San Carlos. Moraga and his officers afterwards took formal possession of the country in the name of Don Carlos Tercero, and the artillery of the Presidio and of the San Carlos, together with the musketry of the troops, proclaimed the birth of Presidio and Pueblo,— the birth of San Francisco. The soldiery, the padres, and the pobladores were then feasted by Moraga, the comandante of the Presidio. The Misión San Francisco de Asís was to have been founded on that saint's day,—October 4th,—but Moraga, with Quirós, the comandante of the San Carlos, and his piloto Cañizares and some of the crew, together with Padre Cambón, were absent upon a survey of the bay. Everything being ready upon the return of Moraga, but without the consent of Rivera, the comandante militar, who was at San Diego, but who was opposed to the foundation, the formal dedication of the Misión with solemn ceremonies took place on October 9, 1776. A procession was formed at the Presidio, and marched thence to the Misión, amid the firing of musketry and the explosion of rockets. Padre Palou officiated as at the founding of the Presidio, assisted by the other padres. Most of the crew of the San Carlos were present, and all the male pobladores. A feast followed, and the Pueblo, the Presidio, and the Misión of San Francisco were now the established northern outposts of Spain in the Californias. (As to the founding of the other misión at the harbor,—Santa Clara de Asís,—see next page.)

## PAGE 59    51/519

Don Fernando de Rivuera = Don Fernando Xavier de Rivera y Moncada.

When the Padre Juan María Salvatierra, the pioneer Jesuit missionary, came to Baja California in October, 1697, and established the Misión Nuestra Señora de Loreto, among his little band of soldiers was a Portuguese named Estevan Rodríguez Lorenzo, who was later, by them, elected their captain. Loyal both to the soldiers and to the missionaries, and a friend to the Indians, his duties soon were in fact those of military governor of the peninsula. When, through blindness, he became incapacitated, his son, Bernardo

Rodríguez, as worthy a man and as good a soldier, succeeded him, but, not inheriting the rugged constitution of his father, he survived him some four years only, dying on December 10, 1750. Enters now upon the scene, as successor of the younger Lorenzo, or Rodriguez, which is probably the patronymic, Don Fernando Xavier Rivera y Moncada, an outstanding figure in the earliest history of the two Californias, and when his name first appears in history he is spoken of as a man thoroughly conversant with the country, and warmly commended for his zeal. He received his commission as comandante of the garrison of Loreto from King Ferdinand VI in 1752. When, on November 30, 1767, Portolá arrived as governor of the Californias, and with orders to expel the Jesuits, he notified Rivera that he was deprived of his commission, and it is stated that Rivera "quietly submitted." When José de Gálvez, the visitador general, arrived on July 5, 1768, he appointed Rivera a comisario, with orders to collect live-stock and supplies from the missions in the peninsula for use at the proposed Franciscan establishments in Nueva California. These were assembled at Velicatá, and Rivera was appointed comandante of the first division of the overland expedition of Portolá. He left Velicatá on Good Friday, March 24, 1769, having with him the Padre Juan Crespi and the pilotín José Cañizares, and arrived at San Diego on May 14th, finding there the San Carlos and the San Antonio, which vessels constituted the sea division of the expedition. Portolá, who commanded the second overland division, arrived on June 29th, and Serra later, on July 1st. Rivera accompanied Portolá on the march to the port of Monterey, proposed as the site of the second Franciscan establishment, being the second in command. This expedition left San Diego on July 14th. The port of Monterey was passed without being recognized, and, the expedition continuing northward, the new port of San Francisco and the Golden Gate were accidentally discovered. Rivera had been ill about this time, and had no part in the discovery. (See note ante, page 103.) On the departure of Portolá from California on July 9, 1770, Don Pedro Fages was appointed comandante militar, and was thus Rivera's superior. The pages of history more than suggest jealousy on the part of Rivera. But Fages was not in sympathy with the padres, and Serra, on his visit to Bucareli in 1773, secured his dismissal, and Rivera superseded him on May 25, 1774. Rivera, who was then in Guadalajara, went to México to receive his instructions, which were comprehensive, and these, with others, were for many years the law in Nueva California. In November, 1774, with Padre Paloú, he went to the Bay of San Francisco on a reconnoitering expedition, but accomplished nothing. (See note ante, page 85.) Rivera went to San Diego after the burning of the buildings of the Misión San Diego de Alcalá and the murder of a padre in November, 1775, during a revolt of the Indians. He punished in different ways some Indians concerned in the atrocities, but the ire of the padres was thoroughly aroused when, sword in hand, with some of his soldiers, he entered a building used for church purposes and seized a ringleader to whom the padres had accorded the right of sanctuary, for which act he and his soldiers were excommunicated. This action of the padres was subsequently approved by Serra and the other padres at Monterey. Rivera was no more acceptable to the padres than Fages had been, and as Portolá had promoted Fages, a teniente, over his head, and as Serra had expressed to Bucareli his preference for José Francisco Ortega, a sargento, as the successor of Fages, the opposition of Rivera to the plans of the padres is understandable. He opposed the founding of the Misión San Francisco de Asís, but he was foiled in this by Serra, when Moraga, Anza's lieutenant, left Monterey with the Sonoran troops and pobladores, to found a presidio and pueblo at the port of San Francisco. Serra sent with Moraga, at this time, the Padres Paloú and Cambón, and Indian servants and supplies,—a separate and distinct equipment from that of Moraga,—and the Misión San Francisco de Asís was founded in defiance of the orders of Rivera. (See note ante, page 106.) Before Rivera left San Diego he received a letter from the Viceroy Bucareli, in which he spoke of the two Franciscan missions at the port of San Francisco as presumably established. This undoubtedly spurred Rivera to action, for when he reached Monterey, although the Padre Presidente Serra was absent, he took with him the Padre Tomás de la Peña, who with the Padre José Antonio Murguía had previously been assigned to the proposed new establishment, and visited the site which had been selected by Padre Tomás, and then proceeded to the Presidio of San Francisco. Rivera and Moraga started out to seek a river seen by the latter earlier in the year. (See note ante, page 106.) It being late in November, they were obliged to turn back on account of threatened high water, and on the way they met a courier with tidings of an Indian uprising at San Luis Obispo, which obliged Rivera to leave hastily for that place. The Padre Tomás was to stay at the Misión San Francisco de Asís until Rivera's return to Monterey, when orders were to be sent up with men and supplies for the founding of the new establishment. The orders were received late in December, and on January 6, 1777, Moraga with a force, and with Padre Tomás, left the Misión San Francisco for the site of the new Misión Santa Clara de Asís, which was dedicated on January 12th by the Padre Tomás de la Peña. On the 21st the Padre José Antonio Murguia arrived with supplies from Monterey. Thus it was that Rivera, who had bitterly opposed the padres in their plans, gave the final order for the consummation of the labors of Bucareli, of Gálvez, of Portolá, of Fages, of Anza, of Serra, to found the two establishments at the new port of San Francisco. But in neither of the Californias was there harmony between the padres and the civil and military authorities, notwithstanding the efforts of Bucareli to effect conciliation; hence changes were made. Felipe de Neve, who, since March 4, 1775, had been acting as governor of the Californias and residing at Loreto, was, on April 19, 1776, regularly appointed as governor by Carlos III, and ordered to make his residence at Monterey, which thereupon became the capital of Las Dos Californias, as it had always been of Nueva California; but Neve's powers were no greater than Rivera's had been. Neve arrived at Monterey in February, 1777. Rivera was made lieutenant-governor of Antigua California, and left Monterey in March, 1777, to make his headquarters at Loreto. He had hitherto been responsible only to the Viceroy, merely reporting to the governor, but now his authority was not so great. On December 27, 1779, he was sent to Sonora and Sinaloa to recruit settlers for the Franciscan establishments, and on his return he was killed while fighting heroically in an Indian uprising, on the Rio Colorado, near the Misión Purísima Concepción (Fort Yuma), July 18, 1781.

PAGE 64 524/56

### Note *e*. Lord Anson's Voyage.

Lord Anson's Voyage Round the World (1740–1744) was published in many editions and translated into most European languages. Lord (George) Anson was born in 1697, of a good family. He entered the navy at an early age, and obtained the command of a fleet commissioned to act against the Spaniards in the Pacific, in 1739. On July 20, 1743, he captured the Manila galleon, sailing from Manila to Acapulco, obtaining booty valued at two and a half million dollars. His voyage was little better than a buccaneering expedition against Spanish trade and settlement, but it was the first step in that career of maritime discovery in which Cook and Vancouver and others earned such laurels, and of the busy colonization to which their discoveries ultimately led. Lord Anson died in June, 1762.

PAGE 65 57/525

### Note *g*. Unas aguas malas, etc.

Although Sir Daines, with his customary conscientiousness when in doubt as to the accuracy of his translation, does not express any such doubt in this instance, yet by setting out the original Spanish in the note he indicates a doubt. His translation, "At the same time you will perceive, that the sea is of an iron color, and looks as if it had small boats, with sails upon the surface," would be more accurately translated, "At the same time, you will perceive that the water is of a purplish color, and resembles small vessels with lateen sails."

# INDEX

Abella, Padre Ramón, one of the founders of Misión San Rafael. See San Rafael.

Academy of Sciences, French (l'Académie des Sciences), 6.

Acapulco, ment., 6; Vizcaíno sails from, in 1602, 95.

Acosta, Martín de. See note on Grijalva, 94.

Adams, Cape. See Cape Adams.

Aguilar, Martín de, search for river bearing his name, 20, 54; note on, 95–96.

Aguirre, Juan Bautista, segundo piloto of the Santiago in 1778, 89; and of La Favorita in 1779, 90; and of the San Carlos in 1775, and seeks Rivera overland expedition from Monterey, 92; names places in Bay of San Francisco, 104.

Agustín, Cabo San, 50. See the large map.

Alaska, Cook surveys its coast, 82; discovered, 99. See Chirikof.

Alcatraz Island, 104.

Aleutian Islands, surveyed by Cook, 82.

Alta California. See California, Nueva.

Alta Loma, 105.

Altimira, Padre José, founder of Misión San Francisco Solano. See Sonoma.

Alzate y Ramírez, José Antonio, 6.

Angel Island, 92, 104.

Anson, Lord (George), biography, 108; his Voyage Round the World, 64, 108.

Anza, Juan Bautista de, instructed to assist Ayala in survey of Bay of San Francisco, 91, 103–104; arrives at Monterey from Sonora in 1774, 94; his connection with the second Bucareli expedition, and his march with troops and pobladores to Monterey, and selection of sites for the Franciscan establishments at San Francisco, 92, 105–106. See note on the San Carlos, 91–93; on Monterey, 93–94.

Archipelago of Saint Lazarus, 48; note, 99.

Arroyo del Puerto, 105.

Arroyo de los Dolores, 105.

Arteaga, Don Ignacio, comandante of the Santiago in 1777, 89; and of La Princesa and of the third Bucareli expedition in 1779, 90.

Assumption Bay (Bahía de Asunción), mouth of Columbia River, discovered by Heceta, 86. ❡ This so-called bay or bahía is the Entrada de Hezeta of the large map accompanying this volume.

Auteroche, Chappe d', his visit to Lower California in 1769 to view transit of Venus, 5; his journey from La Vera Cruz to San Blas, 11; dies at San José del Cabo, 80; his map in Voyage de la Californie, 80.

Ayala, Don Juan Manuel, in command of La Sonora at San Blas, 13; ordered to command of the San Carlos, 15, 92; biography, note, 89–90; voyage to Bay of San Francisco, and survey thereof, 92, 93, 100, 103; his connection with the second Bucareli expedition, 103–105. See Golden Gate; San Carlos, the; Sonora, La. ❡ In several works Ayala's second prænomen (Manuel) is incorrectly given as "Bautista."

Bahía Redondo, 104.

Bahía de Nuestra Señora de Guadalupe, 104.

Bahía de Nuestra Señora del Rosario la Marinera, 104.

Bahía de la Asunción. See Assumption Bay.

Bahía de los Pinos, 94.

Balsa, the Spanish name of the tule canoes of the Indians, 99.

Bancroft, Hubert Howe, his History of the Northwest Coast cited, 81; his reproduced chart of Puerto de la Bodega, 100. See Cape Falcon.

Bay of Biscay, 8.

Bay of Islands. See note De los Remedios, 98.

Bay of Monterey. See note, 93–94.

Bay of San Francisco. See note, 103–106.

## THE END

# NOUVELLES CARTES

## DES DECOUVERTES

## DE L'AMIRAL DE FONTE,

*ET autres Navigateurs Espagnols, Portugais, Anglois, Hollandois, François & Russes, dans les Mers Septentrionales, avec leur Explication ;*

## QUI COMPREND,

L'Histoire des Voyages, tant par Terre que par Mer, dans la partie Septentrionale de la Terre , les Routes de Navigation ; les Extraits des Journaux de Marine, les Observations Astronomiques , & tout ce qui peut contribuer au progrès de la Navigation ; avec la Description des Pays, l'Histoire & les Mœurs des Habitans, le Commerce que l'on y peut faire , &c.

### Par M. DE L'ISLE,

*Professeur de Mathématiques au Collége Royal , Membre des Académies Royales des Sciences de Paris , Londres , Berlin , Stokholm , Upsal , & de l'Institut de Bologne , ci-devant premier Professeur d'Astronomie dans l'Académie Impériale de S. Petersbourg &c.*

# A PARIS,

## M. DCC. LIII.

# VOYAGES

MADE IN THE YEARS 1788 AND 1789,

FROM

CHINA TO THE N. W. COAST OF AMERICA:

WITH

## AN INTRODUCTORY NARRATIVE

OF

## A VOYAGE

Performed in 1786, from BENGAL, in the Ship NOOTKA.

TO WHICH ARE ANNEXED,

OBSERVATIONS ON THE PROBABLE EXISTENCE

OF

*A NORTH WEST PASSAGE.*

AND SOME ACCOUNT OF

THE TRADE BETWEEN THE NORTH WEST COAST OF AMERICA

AND CHINA; AND THE LATTER COUNTRY AND

GREAT BRITAIN.

BY *JOHN MEARES*, ESQ.

VOL I.

*LONDON:*
PRINTED AT THE Logographic Press;
AND SOLD BY
J. WALTER, No. 169, PICCADILLY, OPPOSITE OLD BOND STREET.
1791.

# VOYAGES

## FROM

## ASIA to AMERICA,

For Completing the DISCOVERIES of the

## North West Coast of *America.*

To which is prefixed,

## A SUMMARY of the VOYAGES

Made by the *RUSSIANS* on the

## FROZEN SEA,

In SEARCH of a NORTH EAST Paſſage.

*Serving as an Explanation of a Map of the* Ruſſian *Diſcoveries, publiſhed by the Academy of Sciences at* Peterſburgh.

Tranſlated from the *High Dutch* of
S. MULLER, of the Royal Academy of *Peterſburgh.*

WITH THE ADDITION OF THREE NEW MAPS;

1. A Copy of Part of the *Japaneſe* Map of the World.
2. A Copy of *De Liſle's* and *Buache's* fictitious Map. And
3. A large Map of *Canada,* extending to the *Pacific Ocean, containing the New Diſcoveries made by the* RUSSIANS *and* FRENCH.

---

By THOMAS JEFFERYS Geographer to his Majeſty.

---

## LONDON:

Printed for T. JEFFERYS, the Corner of *St. Martin's-Lane, Charing Croſs,* 1761.

# REMARKS,

In SUPPORT of the

## NEW CHART

OF

## NORTH *and* SOUTH

## AMERICA;

IN

## SIX SHEETS.

By *J. GREEN*, Efq;

L O N D O N:

Printed for THOMAS JEFFERYS, Geographer to his Royal Highnefs the PRINCE of WALES, at the Corner of St. *Martin's-Lane*, near *Charing-Crofs*. MDCCLIII.

# Georg Wilhelm Stellers

gewesenen Adjuncto und Mitglieds der Kayserl. Academie
der Wissenschaften zu St. Petersburg

## Beschreibung
von dem

## Lande

# Kamtschatka

dessen Einwohnern,
deren Sitten, Nahmen, Lebensart
und verschiedenen Gewohnheiten

herausgegeben

von

**J. B. S.**

mit vielen Kupfern

Frankfurt und Leipzig
bey Johann Georg Fleischer 1774

A

# JOURNAL

OF

Captain *C O O K*'s

LAST

# VOYAGE

TO THE

*Pacific Ocean,*

AND IN QUEST OF A

*North-Weſt Paſſage,*

BETWEEN

# ASIA & AMERICA;

Performed in the Years 1776, 1777, 1778, and 1779.

Illuſtrated with a C H A R T, ſhewing the Tracts of the Ships employed in this Expedition.

Faithfully narrated from the original MS. of Mr. *J O H N   L E D Y A R D.*

H A R T F O R D:
Printed and ſold by N A T H A N I E L   P A T T E N,
a few Rods North of the Court-Houſe,
M.D.CC.LXXXIII.

A

# VOYAGE

TO THE

# PACIFIC OCEAN.

UNDERTAKEN,

BY THE COMMAND OF HIS MAJESTY,

FOR MAKING

## Difcoveries in the Northern Hemifphere.

Performed under the Direction of Captains COOK, CLERKE, and GORE,

In His Majefty's Ships the *Refolution* and *Difcovery*; in the Years 1776, 1777, 1778, 1779, and 1780.

IN THREE VOLUMES.

VOL. I. and II. written by Captain JAMES COOK, F.R.S.
VOL. III. by Captain JAMES KING, LL.D. and F.R.S.

Publifhed by Order of the Lords Commiffioners of the Admiralty.

VOL. I.

LONDON:

PRINTED FOR G. NICOL, BOOKSELLER TO HIS MAJESTY, IN THE
STRAND; AND T. CADELL, IN THE STRAND.
M.DCC.LXXXIV.

A

# *VOYAGE ROUND THE WORLD;*

BUT MORE PARTICULARLY TO THE

## NORTH-WEST COAST OF AMERICA:

PERFORMED IN 1785, 1786, 1787, AND 1788,

IN

*THE KING GEORGE AND QUEEN CHARLOTTE,*

CAPTAINS PORTLOCK AND DIXON.

EMBELLISHED WITH TWENTY COPPER-PLATES.

DEDICATED, BY PERMISSION, TO

# HIS MAJESTY.

## By CAPTAIN NATHANIEL PORTLOCK.

*LONDON:*

PRINTED FOR JOHN STOCKDALE, OPPOSITE BURLINGTON-HOUSE, PICCADILLY,
AND GEORGE GOULDING, JAMES STREET, COVENT GARDEN.

M,DCC,LXXXIX.

A

# VOYAGE of DISCOVERY

TO THE

## NORTH PACIFIC OCEAN,

AND

## *ROUND THE WORLD;*

IN WHICH THE COAST OF NORTH-WEST AMERICA HAS BEEN CAREFULLY
EXAMINED AND ACCURATELY SURVEYED.

*Undertaken by HIS MAJESTY's Command,*

PRINCIPALLY WITH A VIEW TO ASCERTAIN THE EXISTENCE OF ANY
NAVIGABLE COMMUNICATION BETWEEN THE

## *North Pacific and North Atlantic Oceans;*

AND PERFORMED IN THE YEARS

1790, 1791, 1792, 1793, 1794, and 1795,

IN THE

DISCOVERY SLOOP OF WAR, AND ARMED TENDER CHATHAM,

UNDER THE COMMAND OF

## CAPTAIN GEORGE VANCOUVER.

*IN THREE VOLUMES.*

VOL. I.

LONDON:
PRINTED FOR G. G. AND J. ROBINSON, PATERNOSTER-ROW;
AND J. EDWARDS, PALL-MALL.

1798.

# NARRATIVE

## OF THE

# ADVENTURES

## AND

# SUFFERINGS

## OF

*SAMUEL PATTERSON,*

EXPERIENCED IN THE PACIFIC OCEAN,

AND MANY OTHER PARTS OF THE WORLD,

WITH AN ACCOUNT OF THE FEEGEE, AND

SANDWICH ISLANDS.

FROM THE PRESS IN PALMER.
MAY 1, 1817.

# VOYAGE

# DE LA PÉROUSE

## AUTOUR DU MONDE,

PUBLIÉ

CONFORMÉMENT AU DÉCRET DU 22 AVRIL 1791,

ET RÉDIGÉ

PAR *M. L. A. MILET-MUREAU*,

Général de Brigade dans le Corps du Génie, Directeur des Fortifications,
Ex-Constituant, Membre de plusieurs Sociétés littéraires de Paris.

## TOME PREMIER.

————————

A PARIS,

DE L'IMPRIMERIE DE LA RÉPUBLIQUE.

AN V. (1797)

*This edition of Francisco Antonio Mourelle de la Rua* VOYAGE OF THE SONORA *was printed in the workshop of Glen Adams, which is located in the sleepy country village of Fairfield, southern Spokane County in Washington state and one township removed from the Idaho line. The text pages were enlarged from the 1920 edition done with hand set Caslon type by Thomas C. Russell of San Francisco. Camera-dark room work was by Sylvia Fenich using a 20x24 inch DS (Japanese) computer driven camera and a 25 inch LogE automatic film processing machine. The old pages were given a 20% enlargement with the camera. The sheets were printed by David Hooper on a 28 inch KORS Heidelberg press. Folding was by Garry Adams using a three stage 22x28 Baum folding machine. Assembly was by the Ye Galleon crew. Paper stock is 80 pound Crest Bark. Binding is by Willem Bosch of Oakesdale, Washington, assisted by William Harnois. The signatures were sewn by Juanita Hurlbert using a National book sewing machine. This was a fun project. We had no special difficulty with the work.*

NAVIGATIO